We do not learn from experience, we learn from reflecting on the experience.

John Dewey

If you say you have a clear conscience then you have a short memory.

Anon

S/he who doesn't recognise the dark in us, as well as the light, is not a fully developed human being.

Veronica Brady

CONTENTS

Author's note
Part One

Writing a Life	1
Writing is memory	3
Opportunity	6
Framework	7
Memoir or autobiography?	10
True stories well told: creative nonfiction	13
The ethics of memoir	17
The writer's voice	19
You have to start somewhere	20
On getting started	22

Part Two

Personal Development	25
The adult male brain	27
On narrative hooks	28
Nature nurture	31
Learned behaviour?	37
On sensory language	40
Sex education	41
A house built on sand	47
Crime wave	56
Endurance	67
Memory	71
Consequences	82
On point of view	87
Discovery	88
Family history	93
The phone call	98
I've had a crook back	101
Financial literacy	105

Part Three

Lessons Well Learnt	115
On a good day	117
Pulling rank	118
On dialogue	124
What it is to be human	125
Working to one's strengths?	132
My brilliant career takes off	135
On descriptive detail	142
Finding a niche	145
Playing make believe	150
On the personal essay	154
Hard roads	155
Corrupting the youth	162
The Ideas Factory	166
March fly lessons	169
Public life	176
Writing by instinct	184
The use and abuse of language	188
Workshops	194
On Show, don't [just] tell	197
Self-portrait	199
More on memoir and life writing	203

Sources — 204

Final Word — 210

In Life There is LUCK

A memoir of an ordinary life with reflections on memoir writing

GRAEME GIBSON

Published by More Than Just Talk

35 Groom Street
Kyogle NSW 2474
AUSTRALIA

www.morethanjusttalk.com.au

© Graeme Gibson 2023

First published 2022

This book is copyright. Apart from any fair dealing for the purpose of private study, research, criticism or review, as permitted under the *Copyright Act*, no part of this book may be reproduced by any process without written permission. Inquiries should be addressed to the publisher.

Cover design and internal layout by Green Avenue Design

Printed and bound by IngramSpark

Cataloguing-in-Publication details are available from the National Library of Australia

A catalogue record for this book is available from the National Library of Australia

www.trove.nla.gov.au

Gibson, Graeme

In Life There is Luck
A memoir of an ordinary life with reflections on memoir writing

ISBN: 978-0-9873196-2-3 (paperback)
ISBN: 978-0-9873196-3-0 (ebook)
ISBN: 978-0-9873196-4-7 (ePDF)

Ingram Spark print on paper sourced from environmentally responsible suppliers.

AUTHOR'S NOTE

I acknowledge the Gullibul people of the Bundjalung nation – the traditional custodians of the land where most of this book has been written – land that was taken without consent, treaty or compensation.

In the creative nonfiction writing workshops I have been presenting since 2013, where memoir is a common interest of participants, I have occasionally been asked, 'Where's yours?' My standard answer of, 'It's coming,' started to wear thin. Threadbare really. So this book is it.

My aim with the book has been to show the value of writing an ordinary life to both the writer, and the greater society, that recognises accomplishment, survival and reflection. This is a conviction I hold strongly. 'The unexamined life is not worth living,' is how the ancient Greek philosopher Socrates put it.

I have seen this value demonstrated many times in the writer and the work they have produced.

Throughout the book I have offered my thoughts on how and why I chose to write in the way I did. I have also written, on occasion, about the personal impact of the writing process. What it means to reveal what had previously not seen daylight.

To protect privacy some names have been changed.

My appreciation goes to the many participants in my workshops who have made me a better writer and a better teacher. For feedback on the manuscript and editorial support I want to thank Margie Brace, Bob Brace and Laurel Cohn.

I also thank Nina, Carlo and Arne Bishop for their part in my life and most of all I want to thank Meg Bishop for her love and support.

PART ONE

Writing a Life

Life writing is inclusive. Everyone has a story of his or her own experience of being in the world. Whatever your achievements or challenges or pain, your story is worth telling – and worth telling in a powerful and absorbing way.

Patti Miller

Writing is memory

Shortly after moving from Canberra to the NSW south coast in 2001, an elderly neighbour let it be known he was having trouble with his computer and wouldn't mind a hand to sort it out. Jack also mentioned he was writing his life story. Turns out the accumulation of saved files was weighing his ancient machine down. Every time he added or changed something in his story, he saved another copy. There were dozens. And, he asked, would we like to have a look at his story? How could you not?

This was a story told as he remembered the events of his life, all of them significant, memorable in some way to Jack. Of the 220 odd pages about 60 dealt with his life before or after his four years of army service during the Second World War, and he was now in his mid-70s. School and billy cart races down the streets of Sydney's Surry Hills, his work as a carpenter, marriage and children, the move from Sydney down the coast – all faithfully recounted. Jack had been working on this for several years and found it immensely rewarding. 'Just doin' it for the family,' he said, 'it won't be a book or anything.'

Writing a life story is one of those things that many people plan to do. One day. For many, that day never comes, but when it does there are many rewards. It can help us understand and put into perspective life's ups and downs, valuing achievements and coming to terms with failures and traumas. It might show someone they are loved, without actually saying so directly. It's personally enriching and finishing the story brings its own rewards.

Writing is memory. Writing about life re-arranges memories, provides new perspectives. The more you write the more you remember, the more side streets, one-way alleys, roundabouts and dead-ends you come to. Life story writing can bring joy and healing, be cathartic and help us find ourselves. It can also stir up and re-surface difficult memories, for the writer, and perhaps others.

The writing may be a straight-forward, simply told tale of personal recollections and family history. It may be written as the writer would speak, speaking at their best, of course. It may be told as it was, or at least as it is remembered, from the point of view of the person the writer once was, as was Jack's approach.

Little time, if any, might be devoted to re-writing, to finding a writing style – a writer's voice. There may be no intention to share the story with anyone other than family and friends. There may be no aspiration to publish for a wider audience. And, as Jack found, this is a perfectly fine, rewarding and admirable achievement. Family and friends will be grateful for the legacy gifted to them. Some may read it.

This is where Jack's story sits on the bookshelf of life writing, which is not to diminish the achievement. If Jack had the interest, time and will he could have created a different type of life story that spoke to a wider audience. On how his life before the army prepared him for war, or not, and how his life was shaped by that service. A reflection on life in Surry Hills as Jack was growing up against the gentrified address it has become would be interesting. This was the setting for Ruth Park's novels, *The Harp in the South* and *Poor Man's Orange*, sagas of several generations living in the poverty of an inner city slum. The changes that came with the move to Jack's coastal idyll would add richness.

Some people want to go beyond the straight-forward simply told tale of their lives and develop their writing skills and style. It is those people I have in mind with this book. Those who want to create something more than the remembered facts of their life.

This may weave together connecting themes and threads through time and place, or be an exploration of an idea or belief that has been a constant throughout their life. It may be an attempt to understand cause and effect. Novelist and essayist E.M. Forster said: 'The king died and then the queen died is a story. The king died, and then the queen died of grief is a plot.' Plot is a narrative with the emphasis on causality. In Forster's simple but elegant example the time sequence is retained but the cause becomes the main story.

Of course, if and when you know more of the story, you might enrich it with relevant descriptive detail; The king died, and then the queen died of grief. Soon after, floundering without its leadership, the kingdom collapsed.

You might add backstory; Some say the king's death was due to the pressure of leading a small kingdom through a recession while being a heavy smoker and paying little attention to his diet.

You might look further, dig deeper; As the kingdom struggled to survive, unemployment skyrocketed, supermarket shelves emptied, relationships were strained and civil unrest followed.

Now it's getting interesting.

You don't need a famous or fascinating life to write a memoir, but setting off on the path to write something for others to read brings an immediate element of gravitas to the effort. On this, American writer, editor and teacher Dinty Moore says;

> Not all writing is political or revolutionary, but the very act of giving yourself permission to write, to speak, to share the truth, no matter whether the truth you understand is a truth others want to acknowledge, is brave, powerful and important.

This book is memoir. It is a collation of a number of short-form writings which are arranged to provide a complete narrative. I'm not famous and my life hasn't been especially fascinating, although I have often been fascinated by events. Like all of us I've had my share of ups and downs with great sorrows and great joys. Chaos and calm. My upbringing was safe but dismal. Many people say they have no regrets. I'm not one of them.

Luck has played a large part in my life, and while I believe it's possible to make much of your own luck, I recognise this is not easy for everyone. Some people are faced with such overwhelming disadvantage making their own luck must seem impossible.

To live a lot you have to risk a little. For me this does not extend to personal safety and health, but it does question the need for personal comfort, complete control over events and perhaps financial security. Along the way I've learnt some things.

All memoir has some element of reflection, otherwise the story becomes a statement of fact, little more than a life resumé. Some parts of this book take on the role of a sociological memoir, unpacking the social, cultural and historical context that shaped events.

I've gone beyond that, to reflect on the actual writing of a memoir. Throughout the book I have offered my thoughts on the how and why I chose to write in the way I have. I have also written, on occasion, about the personal impact of the writing process. And through all of that, my aim has been to show the value of writing an ordinary life, to both the writer and the greater society that recognises accomplishment, ordinariness, reflection and effort. I have seen this value reflected many times, in the writer and in the works they have produced, whether these be short or long pieces. That the writer and the work they produce should be valued, is a conviction I hold deeply.

Opportunity

Early in 2013 I found myself in the north-west New South Wales town of Walgett while my partner was working on a project with the Dharriwaa Aboriginal Elders. The previous several years had been devoted to a local political campaign which I then felt compelled to write a book about, along with building a house. The small business my partner and I ran together in the community, health and environment sectors for many years, had collapsed due to lack of attention. A half-hearted attempt to re-establish it failed, due to lack of enthusiasm. Its time was done. Sitting in Walgett, I pondered, what am I going to do now?

One of our projects, some years before, had been collecting stories of older people's experiences of the environment. These stories, later published in a small book, had arisen from workshops held mostly in public libraries in regional NSW. Later, we were asked to do similar workshops on other themes, again in public libraries. Local history and life story were common themes. I had absolutely loved that work and always wanted to do more. Sitting in Walgett, I wondered if now was the time,

I thought about it a little, took a deep breath, and wandered down to the Walgett library. 'I'm a writer,' I said, 'and I run writing workshops.' The very receptive librarian and I talked a little. Just a little. 'When can you come back,' she asked to my delight. 'And can you go to Lightning Ridge as well?'

From the start I thought I'd be strong at getting people participating in the workshop. That's my background and the approach I take is that people can learn something from me, but they can learn more from and with each other.

I thought I may be a little weaker in the writing bit. Yes, I know it's a *writing* workshop, but I'm being honest here – which is the purpose of memoir. And I've been known to bluff my way through from time to time. To my immense satisfaction (and relief) I found confidence from the start, and that participants were happy with my capacity to deal with the writing aspect.

The workshop I was offering was Life Writing – creative nonfiction for memoir, autobiography, biography, family history, local history, personal essay, travel diary, feature article or whatever people were interested in. From that initial opportunity in Walgett I have built something I find immensely rewarding – helping others. Until COVID 19 changed the world in early 2020 I had given more than 70 workshops in seven years. Each one was different in some way and I always learnt something. It quickly became apparent that memoir was the area most participants were interested in.

Framework

This book had its origins years before its publication. It started with some random memories or questions I had occasionally asked myself, scratched out while taking a flight somewhere or waiting for an appointment. It evolved into an occasional slice of time dedicated to expanding on some of these thoughts. And later on still, it became a project of its own, rather than disconnected pieces. Around that time, it became apparent the book needed a plan, a structure.

The plan was a rough plan, a true mud map, which was intentional. Writing is memory and for me, developing and following a detailed plan would be a blindfold to the possibilities, the revelations I could not have thought of at the initial planning stage. 'Writing is like driving at night in the fog,' novelist E.L. Doctorow said. 'You can only see as far as your headlights, but you can make the whole trip that way.' Of course, different people have different writing processes and for some, a detailed plan will be helpful. Waiting for the fog to lift will be the right approach for them.

Whether the plan be rough or detailed, you might look for pivotal moments and turning points such as when you entered or left a personal relationship, or moved from the big city to a small country town. A mind map, which is a visual representation where you start with a central idea and branch out from there with all related ideas, can help. Brainstorming is not only a group activity but you can do it solo, listing thoughts that come to mind around a central subject before clustering the thoughts. Don't search for important events or people, but focus on what is remembered clearly and vividly.

Structure can take a number of forms. The chronological order of events is how our brain will often want to work and while it is not always the best way to structure the story, it is a useful and easy way to start the writing or planning. You might use this as a default position to get started until a better way becomes apparent. Starting in the midst of things and using flashbacks, or fast forwards are common techniques. A circular or meandering approach and relating the end back to the beginning can be used to close out the story. Chronology is important but it should not rule the roost.

Deep within his novel *Canada*, Richard Ford's character (Del, a writing teacher) offers a broad view of structuring a life story that he presents to his students;

> I try to encourage in them the development of a "life concept"; to enlist their imaginations; to think of their existence on the planet not just as a catalog [sic] of random events endlessly unspooling, but as a *life* — both abstract and finite. This as a way of taking account.

Place your life within the broader society and how it has changed, look for the wider themes, he seems to suggest. Something more than 'random events endlessly unspooling.' So you might structure the memoir thematically. There are often patterns of behaviour or responses to situations that repeat themselves through life. This might be flight or fight in response to challenging situations. It might be your role as peace-maker, or troublemaker. The themes of your life may become most apparent during the process of thinking or writing chronologically.

Viewing your life through a sociological lens offers a broader historical, structural or cultural context. How have your education, working life, political or religious beliefs impacted you? Or others? How have broad societal norms influenced your life? What about your gender or ethnicity? Look for universal themes and big picture issues and examine your personal experiences within them. On that, American writer Vivian Gornick, had this to say;

> A memoir is a work of sustained narrative prose controlled by an idea of the self under obligation to lift from the raw material of life a tale that will shape experience, transform event, deliver wisdom. Truth in a memoir is achieved not through a recital of actual events; it is achieved when the reader comes to believe that the writer is working hard to engage with the experience at hand. What happened to the writer is not what matters; what matters is the large sense that the writer is able to *make* of what happened. For that the power of a writing imagination is required. As V.S. Pritchett once said of the genre, "It's all in the art. You get no credit for living."

Writing your memoir puts you in the position of a tour guide. You decide the route and the itinerary. Where to start, where to stop off, how long for and who you take with you on the journey. This is structural work.

Structure is best found from within the content rather than being allocated before the content is produced. It was only well into the manuscript of this memoir that the structure became apparent. It fell into place when I got hold of a pad of multi-coloured sticky post-it notes and wrote the name of each piece on a note. One piece, one note. Then, on a large empty table, I moved them around. Different pieces called out to other pieces they had connection with. Some demanded separation from other pieces. The chronological order and the thematic nature crystallised. This took place, on and off over several days, before finally they settled into a cohesive tapestry. I, and the pieces themselves I can imagine, heaved a sigh of relief. It was done. I could not have done this at the start, before the writing had commenced.

This opening Part, Writing a Life, is followed by Personal Development which presents some events and turning points that have shaped me. Then comes Lessons Well Learnt, which are exactly that, those events that have had a lasting impact.

When there is a need to indicate a change in direction within the subject, you can use a line break, or a squiggle, or an asterisk as I have done above. Technically, this is called a dinkus.

Memoir or autobiography?

The simplest distinction between memoir and autobiography is that a memoir covers a slice of life while autobiography covers whole of life.

The slice of life we call memoir can be thought of as a zoom lens into limited and specific periods of life, experiences or events. You experience something, have a response to that, and it changes you in some way. Your memoir might be career or family focussed. It may explore an enduring childhood friendship, time spent in prison, or five weeks crossing a desert on foot. This memoir zooms into slices of life, all connected in some way.

Memoir is told from the perspective of the author. It is almost exclusively first person point of view. It should not be a plain re-telling of facts but a narrative that the reader can feel or relate to. Novelistic techniques such as the use of dialogue and the creation of visual images are used. Facts are crucial but so are emotions. The level of personal detail revealed is a matter for the writer. The reader has no entitlement to all the detail.

At its best memoir is not just about the subject but about changes in the subject, their failures, and the wisdom acquired. This is their personal development, a transformative inner journey, known as a character arc.

Writing from the perspective of the person you were and the person you have become – and not necessarily in that order – will add depth and meaning and likely offer a connection with reader's lives, something they can readily relate to. In simple terms, you experience something, learn something about it and about yourself, and develop into something else, finding yourself and your place in the world.

Memoir can be short-form writing, long-form writing or book-length. Short form writing is clear and concise such as short essays or feature articles, opinion pieces, blogs, social media or even Twitter messages. Relating personal experience to current events is common. These pieces can be read in one sitting. Long-form or book-length writing is more detailed and complex. There will be more characters, action and backstory along with exploration of motives and character arc. The narrative will move through time and setting with a beginning, middle and end to the central story that spans the entirety of the work.

Memoir comes from a French word *mémoire*, meaning memory or reminiscence. Most memoir is of people who are not well known publicly, though this can change after publication. Reasons for writing a memoir are many and varied. It might be to contribute to a family or social history. It might be to find yourself, to understand your life, make peace with yourself. Singer and songwriter Bruce Springsteen put it like this;

All I do know is as we age, the weight of our unsorted baggage becomes heavier ... much heavier. With each passing year, the price of our refusal to do that sorting rises higher and higher ...

The whole of life story we call autobiography can be thought of as a wide angle lens. This too is first person point of view, told from the perspective of the author. The author, the narrator and the subject are the same.

Traditionally it was more formal and objective than a memoir, with a greater reliance on fact than emotion. However to a large extent this has changed, and creative storytelling techniques and the character arc are just as important.

Autobiography has a broad scope, examining details of the life being presented in the context of broader issues or events. The author's memory, along with personal records such as letters or photos, is the main source of information. It can be augmented with other people's memories or records. Autobiography comes from the Greek *autos* self, *bios* life and *graphein* to write. Most autobiography is of well-known public figures.

Biography is a story of a life written by someone other than the subject. Unlike memoir or autobiography, it is written in the third person. As with autobiography, a biography covers the whole of a life.

Thorough research is required to ensure accuracy and completeness, necessary to allow fair interpretation and analysis of events, achievements or failures. The subject is usually a public or historical figure. It can be written with or without their approval or support.

Any memoir or autobiography will have greater authority and engender trust in the reader if important information sources are acknowledged, which may be done in an author note. It may also be done throughout the manuscript by using footnotes or endnotes. Memoir though, like all creative nonfiction, uses novelistic techniques and novels do not, as a rule, use footnotes or endnotes. My view is that these add a text or reference-book feel, which I want to avoid. So my sources are acknowledged in a section of that name at the end of the book, referencing the relevant page number.

True stories well told: creative nonfiction

Creative nonfiction comes in many shapes and sizes, including memoir, personal essay, feature article or a poem. It may be short and easily consumed in one reading, or it may be book length. It may be the writer's personal story, a story that can only be told by the individual themselves, such as an account of getting arrested while overseas, or their experience of single parenting. Or it may be a public story on a grander scale or universal theme that could be written by anyone with the time and inclination, as in a review of drug laws or family support services. And it may connect the personal story with the big picture issues of public interest, giving it broader appeal.

More than one person has asked how nonfiction can be creative. Wouldn't that be lying or exaggerating, they ask? Well, no. A creative nonfiction work is factually accurate in its account of real events and people. And it uses the creative techniques of novel writers, playwrights and poets. It is not a text book or an instruction manual.

Using Forster's example of building a plot: 'The king died, and then the queen died of grief,' you can only go into the further detail of the king's lifestyle and the kingdom's collapse, if you know these to be true. If you don't know these details to be true, you must leave them aside, or make it clear this is conjecture. Writing in *You can't make this stuff up*, Lee Gutkind tells us;

> "Creative" doesn't mean inventing what didn't happen, reporting and describing what wasn't there. It doesn't mean that the writer has a license to lie. The word 'nonfiction' means the material is true.

The cardinal rule is clear—and cannot be violated. This is the pledge the writer makes to the reader—the maxim we live by, the anchor of creative nonfiction: "You can't make this stuff up!"

The aim is for a compelling narrative to engage the reader. Dialogue, sensory detail and careful attention to descriptive language are all used. Creative nonfiction is the opposite of journalistic reporting which follows a format known as an inverted pyramid. This is the reporting of what, who, where, when and why. We call this 'the news', as in the following example;

> There has been a single car accident where a late model Toyota sedan crashed into a tree.
>
> The car was driven by Mr Zac Jones with his companion Ms Chloe Myers who were both taken to hospital with minor injuries.
>
> The accident took place in the early hours of Sunday morning with low visibility from heavy fog at the time.
>
> It happened at a notoriously dangerous sharp bend four kilometres from Smithtown heading east.

News reports are written in this way so that if something important happens, such as a sudden change of Prime Minister, the editor of the media outlet can cut paragraphs from the bottom to make more space for the major story, and the report will still make perfect, if brief, sense.

Within the genre of creative nonfiction I have chosen to write in three different but inter-related, or overlapping forms. These are the vignette, flash nonfiction and the personal essay with an occasional poem. I find these suit different situations and different levels of complexity, from the short but remarkable, to the interwoven and life changing. I will explore and explain these different forms here, starting with that most likely to cause panic among damaged learners, of which I was once one – the personal essay.

Forget your schooling or other studies, a personal essay is far less formal, and far less reliant on research than a scholarly essay. It does not follow the traditional scholarly essay structure of an introduction to the main argument (where the reader finds out what the writer is going to say), followed by the evidence in three or four points (where the writer actually says whatever it is), followed by a summary (in which the reader is reminded of what they have just been told).

The personal essay is much more subjective in its writing, being based on the writer's experiences. That is why it's called a *personal* essay. It's an opportunity to tell someone – who you may, or may not know – what you think, perhaps revealing how you think. It is conversational and less structured. It can be pure and plain re-telling of some aspect of a life, or it can stake a claim, make a point of view and justify or argue for it. It can start with little more than a memory, an idea, or a single fact. Or just plain curiosity driven from an observation, a conversation or a media report. The subject can be tackled from all angles. Dig into it and kick it around for a while. See what emerges. Leave it and come back later for a fresh take. It'll look different.

There is an old writer's adage of 'write what you know.' Externally this can be the subject matter or issue at hand. Internally this is the author's response or feelings to that issue, or what they have learnt from an experience. 'Essays,' Australian writer Robert Dessaix has written, 'will be read in 500 years — and the reader will think, *yes,* that's a deeply human thing which I can also feel ... What a wonderful thing is the essay.'

But the adage could also be 'write what you want to know.' Essay comes from the French word *essais,* meaning to attempt or test. It is well suited to try and understand what has happened, or hasn't happened or might happen. Or to test out an idea.

It may be the 800 or so words found in a newspaper opinion piece, often known as an op-ed as it appears (in print versions) opposite the editorial. This is the writer's argument based around their personal or professional experience. There may be a pivotal moment (or two) with bad stuff happening before the sun shines or the case is made. A personal essay may be several thousand words, or it can (rarely) be book length.

In this book I tell a story of mis-adventure in the Small Claims Court, where I was once sued. I follow that story with my experience some years later of working in mediation, which is one way of staying out of the Small Claims Court.

Shorter versions of personal essay depend on a lead: sometimes written as *lede*. A quick opening in the first sentence or two with the aim of the piece becoming clear within the first few paragraphs. The closing must wrap up the argument, being careful that any loose ends serve a purpose.

As the name implies, flash nonfiction is a very short form of nonfiction with a typical word range of 300 to 500, though this may extend up to 1,000. Clearly there may be an overlap with the personal essay, which is of no particular importance. Its focus is the writer's experience of the world, with an emotional element, leaving the reader something to ponder.

Writing such short pieces demands close attention to detail. Every detail. Use the title as part of the story. The opening is critically important and demands to start *in media res*, 'in the midst of things.' There is no space for unnecessary or filler words. Compression is key. Hone in on and magnify one or two essential elements or central images, using specific and concrete detail, sensory language. The ending doesn't have to be at the end, but make the last lines memorable. Don't tell the reader what to think, but give them something to think about.

The vignette is a short impressionistic sketch focussed on one or two specific moments, characters or details. Pronounced vin-yet, and taken from the French word 'vigne' meaning little vine, it is a little story of probably no more than a few hundred words. It uses sensory detail and imagery to present a graceful account.

The vignette may be a stand-alone piece, or it can provide an opportunity within a story to move away from the main narrative, zoom in on, highlight and closely examine one particular character, place or moment.

The ethics of memoir

… or, being honest, not losing friends and staying out of court.

Memoir, like all writing, must establish trust in the reader. It has to be believable, and it should be authoritative, which anyone writing their memoir should be able to manage. Showing your own vulnerabilities, weaknesses and failures will help establish trust. This is your writer's voice, with its thoughts and feelings attached to your history and experiences. As a guiding principle I say be hard on yourself, exposing the warts, and be gentle on others. Doesn't mean you shouldn't say someone was a bastard if you think they were, and if you want to, but provide the context, the nuance, and own it as your opinion. Be compassionate towards the bastard, consider their point of view.

Revenge might make a good plot, but it's a terrible motive. You might well find your writing cathartic, but will others find it narcissistic or self-justifying? Are you writing a confessional? These are questions to be thought through. But, most importantly, how do you write about your life, which will include other people, when some of those people may not appreciate what you say about them, or may be outright hostile?

Put it all down in a complete first draft. This is best done quickly, without attention to detail, just getting it down. Don't jump at shadows, don't worry about the reactions of others while you write. You are writing for yourself, not them. You might think of it as a private draft. Leave it a healthy length of time and return to it asking what it's really about. Is it relevant? Is it honest and fair?

From first and early drafts it's likely some content will not be included in the final manuscript. It may be too revealing, too personal. It might make the people who matter to you uncomfortable, unhappy or angry, with a risk of relationship damage. It might cause you emotional damage. Secrets that others have shared with you should be off-limits. We all know the truth can hurt, so is it a truth worth telling? Is there a balance between maintaining the peace (or keeping a lid on the simmering tensions) and being true to yourself? Remember, once it's in print – including on-line – it's there forever.

Even that which you decide to delete will, in some way, influence your thinking and your writing. In this memoir I have closely considered the manner in which I have recorded events that involve others. Some passages have been re-worked extensively. Some have been excluded, but I'm glad I wrote them.

It may not be until the draft is complete that it becomes clear some of this writing is not appropriate for a general audience. That doesn't mean the work has been a waste in any way – it has likely served its purpose for the writer.

You might show particular passages to people who were involved and seek their response but how you deal with that will be a decision for you. Be clear beforehand whether you are seeking feedback, are willing to negotiate, or are offering a right of veto. Changing a word or phrase can alter meanings and inferences and be a salve to someone's bruises. But remember also, this is your memoir. Others can write theirs if they choose.

While you don't have to reveal everything, you need to question how much to hold back. Your memoir may be about abuse but you decide how much detail to reveal. Ask yourself also, why write memoir if your first impulse is to keep it to yourself?

Memory is fallible and unreliable, selective and subjective, rarely objective. Memoir is a selection of life's events and by necessity a selective re-telling. Many decisions are made along the way about the selection of events, the sequence in which these events are re-created, and the emphasis given to these different events.

You are not writing a text book, or a manual. This is not straight journalistic reporting of facts but a literature of reality with drama, humour and emotion written in good faith.

Before self-publishing *Beyond Fear and Loathing: Local politics at work*, I had the manuscript reviewed by a defamation barrister. In those instances where I was stating something that someone was likely to disagree with, the advice was to clearly include the other person's point of view. In that book, the other person was a local council mayor, well known for threatening legal action.

I interviewed the mayor to confirm his position on a couple of issues, amended the text as appropriate and then published, fully expecting a letter from the mayor's legal representative demanding a public retraction and the burning of all remaining copies in the town square at midday following. That letter never came.

There is a parallel in memoir, where you might say it how it was from your point of view, but then clearly show another point of view. 'This is how I saw it. However, my cousin/ sibling/ former prison cell-mate/ neighbour saw it like this…'

But please don't take this as legal advice. It is not. If you are concerned you might run into problems, consult an expert.

The writer's voice

The voice a writer adopts is important to all writing. It needs to be authoritative, trustworthy and able to keep a reader's interest. In life writing this is critical, as the author is telling a true story from their personal point of view. No-one else is going to see things, interpret things and experience things *exactly* as the author has. This is very personal and often idiosyncratic as the author exposes themselves, allowing the reader to follow their mind at work, with all its genius and vulnerability.

A writer's voice may take on a range of different tones. For example, it may be humorous or serious, philosophical or whimsical, detached or affected, reasonable or strident. It will choose and arrange words and phrases to make sentences. And then paragraphs. It may follow the proper rules of grammar, or it may loosen the strictures.

This first part of the book has ranged broadly over a number of aspects of life writing and creative nonfiction. It has provided a glimpse of the approach I have taken, which I have put into practice in the following two parts. But first, a little on starting out.

You have to start somewhere

>Write in a reckless fever. Rewrite in a cardigan.
>
>**D.B.C. Pierre,** *Release the Bats: Writing Your Way Out Of It*

Many people say that getting started in writing, or any other activity, whether creative or mundane, is the hardest part. They are right, of course. Procrastination and me are old friends, so I know this. But there are ways it can be overcome.

The right side of your brain is said to be the creative side, the left side the analytical side. Your spellchecker, inner editor and self-critic live in the left side. Both sides have a time and a place. Getting started is not the time or place for the left side. Be aware.

Start by starting, in full acceptance of doubts, uncertainties and lack of control. Spelling, grammar and logic are unimportant. Find something to write about and write. Known as free writing, or stream of consciousness, the intention is to keep the pen moving, or the keyboard busy, without stopping to re-read what you have just written.

The aim here is quantity, not quality. Productivity, not brilliance. It's about getting it out. The professional writerly term for this is a vomit draft. It will be messy, unattractive and maybe smelly. But within the pile will be some image or truth, some gem worth polishing. Maybe more than one.

The following piece is included as an example of getting started – quantity, not quality, stream of consciousness writing. I hand wrote it to get it out of my system and it flowed seamlessly, with no self-prodding to stop and think about it, or re-read. It will contribute to something else on a nature theme I have planned as a future project.

I came home the other day to a bleak scene. A very bleak scene. Our neighbours, an elderly couple with mobility problems and unable to get up the steep slope that forms their backyard and adjoins the steep slope that forms our backyard had gotten the tree cutters in and had the lilly pillie's, the mango and jacaranda trees and a few other smaller things cut down and I mean cut down, almost to ground level not just pruned, which was not pleasing to our eyes and I struggle to see how they could find it pleasing to their eyes, as where once was a verdant scene, with elkhorns, fruit for the birds and bats and a splash of mauve flower to fill a stormy sky, now there was nothing and to eliminate any arboreal resistance they had the tree cutter come along with their stump grinder and take it all, and I mean all for now there is only a smatter of bark chip after this, an act of stupidity, of bastardy, and never mind our neighbours saying it was too hard for them to get up the slope and look after the trees, a backyard mango doesn't need looking after and nor does a mature jacaranda, and if they ever did then some thoughtful pruning might be all that is needed, and a whole lot cheaper than having them 100 per cent removed, and after all this I keep thinking about our neighbour who told us soon after we moved in how he had planted those trees, many decades ago and how he liked the birds, though probably not the bats as they are less popular around here, but what were they thinking, where will the frogmouths perch?

And the next day, when it's time for a new sentence, I'm still feeling bad about this. Before I know it though, the tree cutter is back and takes out a cycad from the front yard. And this cycad had a trunk taller than me and I'm a six footer, plus a bit, in old measure. We hear later of the problems that came from the cycad scratching the neighbours as they get the mail. But the letter box is nowhere near where the cycad was. Was.

Reminds me of another instance, long ago in another place, where an elderly lady sought, and was granted, permission to have a mature tree in her yard cut down because the birds, you see, that sat in that tree, made a mess on her rubbish bin, that she stored under that tree. Birds. Tree. Rubbish. Shit.

And, now, a little later, I'm still disappointed. These neighbours of ours are good and decent people. OAM one of them likes to put after their name. I'm sure they've been called salt of the earth and I wouldn't dispute that. I spend a lot of time trying to understand why people do what they do, it's part of my work. And I understand private property rights, but only a certain worldview would go for the clear felling option, as our neighbours have done, and I can't fathom that. I just can't.

On getting started

Think of the grain of sand or grit that gets within an oyster shell, causing irritation, which brings a defensive response from the oyster. It starts to cover the intruder with layers of nacre. This is the same material that forms the oyster's shell but it is only the annoyance of the intruder that leads to the brilliant iridescence we know as a pearl. The annoyance of poking your memory or forcing yourself to write might lead to something equally valued. And it might not take as long as a pearl takes to grow.

> All artists work to acquire and perfect the tools of their craft, and all art involves evaluation, clarification, and revision. But these are secondary tasks. They cannot begin (sometimes they must not begin) until the *materia*, the body of the work, is on the page or the canvas.
>
> **Lewis Hyde,** *The Gift*

Evaluation has no place in the initial creativity of the vomit draft.

Everyone has heard the sayings 'go with the flow,' or 'being in the zone.' Psychologist Mihaly Csikszentmihalyi added some weight with his study of the state he calls 'flow.' In simple terms the study, based on dozens of interviews with tradesmen, chefs, artists and others, describes the state of flow as being completely absorbed in something that requires effort but is not a struggle. Time slips and a sense of great satisfaction is had at the end result. Flow is readily lost when we stop to re-read what we have just written.

Having difficulty starting, or getting stuck in the middle of some writing have the same consequences. It's called writer's block, which Ernest Hemingway had an answer for: 'All you have to do is write one true sentence. Write the truest sentence that you know.' When you have written that one true sentence you are away, unblocked. Just keep adding to it.

Writing is memory, I said earlier. The more you write the more you remember, the more avenues for exploration arise. Tangents are our friends. Even in the crude form of a vomit draft your writer's voice becomes evident. Your personal history or experiences, with the attached thoughts and feelings come through.

PART TWO

Personal Development

Memoir requires transcendence. Something has to happen. Or shift. Or merely move. Someone has to change a little. Or grow. It's the bare hack minimum of memoir.

Marion Roach Smith

The adult male brain

They say the adult male brain doesn't fully develop until around age 25 and I was only 21, on this particular Saturday morning. A Saturday morning unlike any other.

Home alone, pacing the flat, a soul-less two-bedder in Darwin's northern suburbs. Out to the verandah, with Darwin airport's main runway in the distance, where the Jumbos came and went. It had been less than a year since I had first landed there, from the south. Through the flat, inspecting its meagre furnishings, the possessions, clothes, a few books. A radio for company, distraction. A telephone stubbornly refusing to ring. Back out to the verandah. Round and round. Inside, outside.

Feeling vaguely nauseous, not so much dread as a little bit dead, the question repeated itself; How had it reached this stage? At the time, I had no answer. I just knew I didn't want to do this. Later, years later, it became clear. I lacked the skills to take control, to navigate the situation, to find a path forward with optimism. To start the mature conversation the situation had demanded months earlier. To change things at this late stage would be to create a situation I couldn't face. There would be grief, tears, drama.

At the time I felt alone in the world. Though I have long since known my experience was not unique. Resigned to the situation, on that Saturday in October 1976, I knew I had left it too late. There was nothing else for it but to go off and get married. There would be consequences.

This stark scene from the account of my marriage works as a narrative hook, a literary technique to engage the reader early and maintain their interest, but it's so bleak I struggled with whether or how to use it at as an opening. It took many revisions until I found a tone I was comfortable with, from a personal and an ethical point of view.

An opening to any form of creative writing aims to engage the reader quickly. Then and there. With so much choice for reading and so little time, the reader's interest or imagination must be piqued early. Everyone has been turned off reading an article or a book by an opening that falls flat, or confuses.

The narrative hook might create suspense, establish atmosphere or promise things to come. It can set up character and situation, establish a point of view or point to an emotional state.

The opening may be a sentence, a paragraph or a number of pages. But get straight to it with sharp language, avoiding writerly throat-clearing. As with fishing, the sooner the hook is set, the better.

A narrative hook may be a fact about yourself, something central to your life. It may be an anecdote that reveals something significant. It may be a guiding thought you aim to live by or a personal observation that relates to wider society. Or it may be something else.

On narrative hooks

Some openings you may see elsewhere in this book;

> Fact
>
> During those wasteful high school years my parents would occasionally talk about the importance of a career. As a wilful youth I would ask why they wanted to talk about that place over near China.
>
> Anecdote
>
> Mavis had this thing about keeping the family's dirty washing out of view: 'No-one's business but ours,' she'd say whenever some trouble or other came up. And some trouble had come up one warm summer night, when I was about ten.
>
> Thought
>
> It's better to go down the wrong street than stand on the corner.

Observation

There is a well-established link between child abuse and neglect and delinquent behaviour.

Whatever incident, character or theme is used in a hook, it must be honoured. It must have a part in the story that follows. Red herrings are not welcome. Icebergs, the tip of the story, allude to some far bigger conflict or growing relationship tension, out-of-view for the time being.

Beginning in the midst of things, known as *in media res*, as I mentioned earlier, does away with the descriptive explanation by bringing some critical element to the start. This is commonly used to good effect. Some openings that use *in media res*;

> One warm April evening in 1984, in a pleasant suburb of Cairo called Zamalek, three exquisite young men tried to kill me. A dance with knives and a pricking at the throat that began with a coffee at Groppi's and ended, not with a severed wind-pipe, but, oddly enough, with my finding a voice.
>
> **Robert Dessaix,** *A Mother's Disgrace*

> I'm flying down the Hume Highway at 130 kilometres an hour. I've lost control a few times but the *brrrr* of those white guide things on the side of the roads keep me on track. A steering wheel wet from tears is a very slippery object. I am sobbing uncontrollably. *Will he even recognise me? If he doesn't I'm going to just turn around and walk the other way.* I haven't seen my father in nine years. Since I was thirteen in fact.
>
> **Anh Do,** *The Happiest Refugee*

It is quite common to find your opening when a draft of the story is complete, or nearly so. Only when you have it down do you clearly see the range of possible openings, such as the option to bring a key point forward, from 'the midst of things,' to the opening.

More or less chronological openings can also work well;

> I arrived in the Alice at five a.m. with a dog, six dollars and a small suitcase full of inappropriate clothes. 'Bring a cardigan for the evenings,' the brochure said. A freezing wind whipped grit down the platform and I stood shivering, holding warm dog flesh, and wondered what foolishness had brought me to this eerie, empty train station in the centre of nowhere.
>
> **Robyn Davidson,** *Tracks*

In memoir or autobiography, starting with, 'I was born in …' is not recommended. But as with most things, there are exceptions. It works for Clive James who opened *Unreliable Memoirs* with: 'I was born in 1939. The other big event of that year was the outbreak of the second world war, but for the moment that did not affect me.' The opening short sentence is countered by the longer second sentence revealing a quirky style, an apparent self-centredness.

And it worked for Bert Facey whose book, *A Fortunate Life*, opens with: 'I was born in the year 1894 at Maidstone in Victoria.' The simply told tale of Facey's extraordinary life, has sold more than one million copies since being first published in 1981.

Some openings hint at, or provide a direct link to something deeper, a particular emotional state;

> We had always been close. He took me with him sometimes on short trips when I was very small, driving along the railway line from Finke because it offered a better, though bumpier, route than the sandy track through the dunes. I

divined my specialness to him early, and it was precious to me. When the drinking began to affect his moods I still felt the specialness, but with it a responsibility to something dark and sad that surfaced in him.

Kim Mahood, *Craft for a Dry Lake*

He stood behind the front door of his grandfather's house, with a pitchfork held tightly in both hands, knowing that he would probably kill his uncle if he forced his way into the room.

Raimond Gaita, *Romulus, My Father*

Nature nurture

In psychology there has long been a nature versus nurture debate about aspects of human behaviour.

Nature comes from the genes and hereditary factors that influence our personalities and physical appearance. These are traits inherited from our biological parents. An evolutionary hand-me-down, if you like. Nurture comes from environmental variables and our life experiences including our lifestyle choices: it is conditioning from our upbringing and societal culture that shape us.

For many years debate centred on the relative significance of nature and nurture, the importance of one over the other, with dedicated supporters in both camps. The now widely accepted view is that both nature and nurture interact throughout our lives. Which seems so obvious you could wonder why there was any debate in the first place. Then again, the world was once thought to be flat.

We may be born into a family of tall parents and older siblings, where our genetic inheritance suggests we too would grow tall. But if we experience famine and poor nutrition during our developmental years, we may not grow as tall as otherwise. We could say we were poorly nurtured.

Lower back problems are with me. The nature part of the equation would suggest this is in part because of my: '... congenitally narrow lumbar canal due to short pedicles.' Diagnosis from an MRI scan confirms this. The nurture part of the equation would point to my earlier days, when I was young, silly and invincible. The two parts interact. If I had treated my body better when younger, the short pedicles I was born with, along with the rest of my back, may have behaved better later on.

I imagine nature has provided me with average intelligence, but there were few moments in my upbringing or schooling that provided much nurture. The zest for learning was not planted. Inspiration was in short supply. It was only some years after school that, subconsciously, I took charge and nurtured my own learning.

Number One Maria Street Edwardstown was the conventional 1950s Adelaide household I was born into. As was the norm, my father, Wallace Pax (known to all as Pax), was the bread-winner. Mavis, my mother, gave up paid work shortly after Pax returned from service in World War Two. I have two older siblings, one ten years older than me, the other five years older. Good spacing you might say.

There was also a grandfather, on Pax's side, who had lived with my parents from the time they were married (or very soon after) until his death when I was 16. His wife, my grandmother, had died the year I was born after a long illness. Mavis had a major responsibility to look after her ailing mother-in-law, from, I think, the start of her married life. Few other extended family members were part of my orbit. We saw Mavis's father and her two sisters occasionally. There were a couple of cousins, but I barely knew them.

Our Edwardstown house, eight kilometres or so from the city centre, was an old blue-stone with a few Besser block add-ons, complete with the latest aluminium windows, on a one-acre block. The block had a clay tennis court but this was in total disrepair by the time my memory developed. No Sunday afternoon tennis for me. The many almond trees provided some pocket money from sales at the nearby Ditters factory, and on a scruffy acre there was always somewhere to hide out on your own.

Edwardstown had a couple of parts to it. The residential area to the east and the commercial and industrial area, along, and to the western side of South Road. The residential area is mostly well gentrified now. In 1989, well after I had left, the residential area changed its name from Edwardstown to Melrose Park. Very uppity.

When I was 15 my parents, along with a reluctant grandfather and I, their equally reluctant youngest child, moved to a house they had built at Eden Hills, a few kilometres to the south. Eden Hills, I thought at the time, sounded very snobby, and Edwardstown kids didn't do snobby. I preferred to say it was near Blackwood, a much less grandiose sounding name. And here I stayed most of the following years until at age 20, with life skills in sharp deficit, I eagerly accepted a two year job transfer to Darwin and whatever adventure that would bring.

On leaving, going through the ritual farewells to parents, siblings, my loose friendship group, I knew just one thing with absolute certainty. I would not be returning to Adelaide in two years.

When constructing a memoir (which I mentioned earlier comes from the French, meaning memory or reminiscence) there is a need to sieve the memories. Just because something happened, doesn't mean it's interesting. And just because it might be interesting, doesn't mean it belongs. Memories that serve the overall narrative earn their place.

In thinking back on my childhood, the memories that come to mind most vividly are not joyful. They paint a less than rosy picture, but these are my experiences, my recollections. That they come to front of mind stems from the human brain having a greater sensitivity to bad news, unpleasant events and upsetting experiences. Even when events are of similar intensity, negative events have a greater effect on our psychological state than positive or neutral events. This is known as negativity bias and it extends to memories of past events. It explains why being criticised has more impact than being praised. It explains why negative political campaigns are effective. For me, and this writing, it is clear that the troughs of my negative experiences were deeper, and remain more vivid, than the peaks of my positive experiences. I have come to terms with this. This is not to say there was no happiness. But it was more fleeting than prolonged.

Large life-changing events only happen occasionally. I opened this part of the book with one of them, a reflection on the hours before my marriage. The small moments of regular life come around much more frequently and can equally change us. Capturing the small moments of life in writing needs a sharp and observant eye for specific detail, to note significant dialogue, and capture the feel of the scene though a dominant sense. This is a writing skill worth developing.

The story I have just told, of my Adelaide upbringing, opens with the big picture of human behaviour before connecting with the physical and familial environment I grew up in. It then closes with a reference back to human behaviour, specifically the inescapable prioritisation we give to memories. Linking the opening with the closing provides a sense of completion to the story. A full circle.

The opening and closing are analytical, observant. The personal experience sandwiched between is flash nonfiction, which I found well suited to capture the specific detail and raise a few ponderables in the 450 words that have a clear form, with a start and a finish.

For a change of pace, to add variety, I am now presenting a few stark and clear memories about my mother, from my early upbringing. These are told in four vignettes, sparse but specific in their detail. These things have probably not happened to you, but you may know exactly what the experience felt like.

The first vignette is a story of humiliation, and I am its illustration. This approach to memoir writing is taken from *The Memoir Project* by Marion Roach Smith.

1. Picture this.

A primary school on a cold, wet winter's day with the chip heater of the weatherboard classroom working double time. Lunch was to be had in the classroom. The class teacher – name forgotten, middle aged woman – was providing an extra-curricula lesson in communality. We were asked to share our sandwiches.

Along with all the other kids, I put mine out on the big table. All white bread, with vegemite a stand out. Fritz (you have to be South Australian) and sauce, or cheese from the blue packet were common.

Mrs Forgotten-her-name looked at mine, with no obvious filling. She lifted a lid to inspect. 'Sugar,' she gasped. 'You've got sugar sandwiches! Well you can't share them. You'll have to have them yourself.'

And that's what I did. Sitting quietly on my own, wishing it wasn't so.

Mavis was stubborn but not normally cruel. She probably thought Mrs Forgotten-her-name was out of order, but there were no more sugar sandwiches after I shared my experience at home later that day.

I don't know that Mavis was much given to thinking about cause and effect, but less than ten years later I recall her being kind, as I had a couple of days off school while a partial denture was fitted. There is no resentment and I'm not complaining. How could I, when you hear stories of young people living in remote locations, such as Bass Strait islands, having all their teeth removed – as a precaution – so they don't get toothache!

For many years, unable to acknowledge the reality, I explained my false teeth were the result of a wayward knee playing football. I claim the reality now, rather than the falsehood. It wasn't football, my front teeth were rotten.

2. While I don't remember Mavis's words, I remember clearly the snarl in her voice. I do remember Pax's words though: 'Take it out on me, but don't

take it out on the kids.' I was about eight when this took place, early on a Sunday before a planned picnic, an event that had been spoken of several times during the week. I was alone at the door of my parents' bedroom during this exchange. Mavis was in bed, which was where she stayed.

So off we went, father and youngest child. I remember Pax wore a cravat. There was a sausage, or perhaps a lamb chop on a barbeque somewhere. We called in on a few parks in the Adelaide hills, played some French cricket. And I remember he cried, on and off, throughout this long and wretched day.

I have no idea what the argument was about. No explanation was offered, no soothing consolation provided to an anxious child, for that was the way things were done. I don't know what I thought, whether the situation was going to pass or to become entrenched. But I remember it clearly.

3. My sister, ten years older than me, married when I was nine or ten. Shortly after this, she and her husband were planning a move to Melbourne. There was tension around this, tension I didn't understand. And arguments.

One night in the kitchen Mavis told me that next time my sister visited she wanted me to tell her I had overheard Mavis and Pax talking about taking my sister out of their will. I didn't know what a will was. Mavis explained. 'And do it good,' she said. 'Start crying when you tell her.'

I didn't do Mavis's bidding. I may have known right from wrong, or doubted my acting skills. It was only years later that I wondered how she could have been so manipulative, to try and use one child as a weapon against another.

I write this without rancour. Mavis was a product of her own upbringing and circumstances. I can well imagine her justifying it to herself, in her black and white worldview, 'Well I had to do something.' But she wasn't always a nice person.

4. 'You said what?' was Mavis's exclamation when I returned from the corner shop with the remnants of a Wagon Wheel in hand. This was suburban Adelaide circa 1964 where no-one lived far from a corner shop. Whenever I had sixpence I'd be off to the shop for a Wagon Wheel, a delicious chocolate coated circular disc of tooth decay.

'Shippy' was the shop owner, a jovial, avuncular fellow. I don't know his name and I'm not sure anyone did. It may have been Shipworth or something like that. I must have been a bit cheeky from time to time. Certainly Mavis thought I'd gone too far advising Shippy that his real status in life was that of a public servant. He was, after all, there to serve the public, and it seemed a fair description to me. Later in the day when Pax returned home, I was hauled up to the shop and made to apologise. Quite embarrassing, but I learnt not to boast of my exploits to Mavis.

Years later I heard that Shippy provided another public service to local youth. Buying their beer from the local while they were under age. However, I was some time away from availing myself of that service.

As was common for that time, my childhood was under the doctrine of, 'Wait till your father gets home,' to mete out the punishment. Unlike some kids I knew, my punishments were never severe. I never experienced anything that could be describes as a flogging. Unlike some kids.

Learned behaviour?

Closing the previous vignette on childhood misdemeanours and parental discipline with 'Unlike some kids …' presents the opportunity to build on the theme, to go deeper and broader, which I have done here with a personal essay on child abuse. This connects the personal – my observed experience, with the universal – the long-term impact of that abuse.

Mavis had this thing about keeping the family's dirty washing out of view. 'No-one's business but ours,' she'd say whenever some trouble or other came up. And some trouble had come up one warm summer night, when I was about ten. I had been out in the street with my best mate Mark, doing what had become something of a regular habit: lobbing small rocks onto the tiled roof of the Curtis's house on the corner.

We didn't like them ever since old man Curtis complained about us riding our bikes over the new shoots of his freshly sown Yates *Adelaide-blend* lawn on the nature strip, leaving deep furrows. They were new to the street and we thought they were big-noting themselves trying to have a fine lawn like that out the front. No-one else did. Truth be told, to a couple of mischief makers like us, the length of string tied to some tomato stakes marking out the no-go area was more invitation than deterrent.

All of a sudden Pax appeared, called me inside and sent Mark home. His tone said something was up so I dropped my handful of gravel and quickly did as told. Inside, Mavis bellowed I had 'really done it now'. Pax explained there had been a phone call from the sergeant at Edwardstown Police Station. 'Your son is out on the street throwing rocks onto a neighbour's roof,' the sergeant had informed my startled father. 'I'm coming down. Get the boy inside, I want to talk to him.'

While we waited the interrogation started. 'Why? Who did I think I was? What if one of the stones accidentally went through a window and hurt someone? What would the other neighbours think?' Mavis was the chief interrogator and I'd been through this before. Her favourite tactic to overcome the sullen response I'd perfected was to repeat the question. She chain-smoked Hallmarks and never tired. Pax had little to say but thought I should have known better. I don't think he liked the Curtis's either. They both concluded I had been led astray by Mark because his parents often argued, loudly, and his father drank too much. After a while Pax went out to the shed to do something.

Half an hour or so later he came back in and said he didn't think the police sergeant was coming down after all. He thought it must have been Mr Curtis who had made the phone call to scare us and get me sorted out. I think Pax saw the funny side to this but it made Mavis angrier. In our family, shame was a monster, and she reinforced the potential for shame I had created. I was not to talk about this disgraceful episode with anyone and was made to give a solemn promise not to repeat the offence. And that was it for me. My mate Mark – guilty of the same offence – got one hell of a flogging from his father. I recall the purple welts on his legs. He didn't talk to me for days.

That was not the only time Mark suffered at the hands of his violent father, and I suspect, cowed but complicit mother. I well remember coming back to Mark's house one Sunday afternoon, quite late. We had been out somewhere with their family dog, a bitzer called Winston. As we approached the front door Mark's mother called out: 'Is that you Mark?' And I remember, as if it was yesterday, her quick follow-up, the anguished and priority setting: 'Where's Winston?' Next second the father was out, slapping Mark around the head without restraint. I have no idea how frequent this sort of punishment was meted out. Mark didn't say. But I remember Mark barely uttered a sound during this assault. Perhaps he was very familiar with this.

I know Mark was interfered with. He sold newspapers after school, outside a nearby factory before moving around to the local hotels. At the factory he waited inside the security shed for the four o'clock shift to finish. And in that grim little shed, each day, waited the friendly old bloke with the proverbial bag of lollies. The friendly old bloke with the hands he couldn't keep to himself. I know. I was there once. I don't know the extent of the abuse; I never went back and Mark and I never talked about it. Certainly there was no-one in my life's orbit that I could talk to about this.

There is a well-established link between child abuse and neglect and delinquent behaviour. In adulthood this extends to antisocial, violent and criminal behaviour. Children who are sexually abused are around five times more likely to commit crimes as adults. That some of those sexually abused children continue to suffer abuse, or psychological stress, or become perpetrators themselves in adulthood, is well known.

If the initial abuse or neglect is a form of punishment, a loss of innocence, then that punishment may continue through to the adult years. And for some, it's a virtual life sentence.

Bikes and tadpoles and cricket on the street might form part of the metaphor for the idyllic suburban childhood of 1960s Australian suburbia, but this wasn't every child's reality.

Mark grew into a deceitful and cheating friend, which, I imagine, was the only way he knew how to survive his family. We drifted apart. A couple of years later we went to separate high schools, drifting further. When I was 15 my parents and I moved to a different suburb. About this time, as soon as he was allowed, Mark left high school. I never saw him again, but a few years later I saw his elder sister at a party. Diane told me he'd moved out of home early and had been continually in trouble with the police.

I have long since moved away from Adelaide and have no connections there. Still, I occasionally wonder what became of Mark, about the early patterns in his home life and how this affected his life decisions. Was there some sort of recovery and discovery of an equilibrium? Did he form satisfying relationships? Or did he practice what he had learnt, repeating the brutality? After all, hurt people hurt people.

On sensory language

Whether consciously or sub-consciously we experience the world through our senses. The use of physical and emotional language transfers the experience into a sensory realm. It brings richness and depth and tempts the reader's imagination. It allows readers to experience the world you are writing about and connect with the story, to see the image or scene. In the previous piece I tried to capture the feel of my experience of child abuse through sensory language.

Sensory language connects to the five senses of sight, sound, smell, taste and touch. This can be direct or through trigger words and phrases that appeal to the sense.

Direct words for sight would typically describe or refer to colour, shape, size and overall appearance. The sight sense could be triggered by reference to a summer time heat haze. Or the bleached grasses of the inland plain. Or something else. 'I am not going out with you dressed like that,' she said, as he pulled on his red swimmers for the late afternoon walk to the pool. Red swimmers. To go with the red floral shirt he had worn all day.

For sound, direct words are what we hear, such as loud, quiet, melodic or rhythmic. This can be triggered through suggestive words, such as soothing, grating or raucous. Like a kookaburra.

Smells can be strong, faint, sweet, sickly or acrid. Or the sense of smell can be triggered through suggestion, such as cut grass, fresh sex, rain on dry earth or a wet dog.

Sweet, sour, bitter and salty are the common modes of taste that can be directly referenced. These might be triggered through mention of specific foods such as mint, lemon, chili or vodka.

Sensory language referencing touch includes words such as wet and dry, smooth and tough, cool and warm. This can be triggered through images of silk, wool, ice or sandpaper. Perhaps the tentative first touch of two knees under the table. In *Celebration of the Senses*, Eric Rolls writes of a chance encounter with a brown snake as he is on hands and knees inspecting the fittings of a water tank: '… sixty centimetres of scales scraped my ear before I rolled clear. I know forever the feel of an angry snake.'

A reader's response might be deepened if you avoid naming the sense. The rain didn't sound heavy on the roof, for example, but it made its presence felt. Nothing as fresh as the air you breath after diving through a cold wave in an early morning swim. A personality as bland as a choko.

Sex education

Sexuality is an important part of life, bringing joy, misery, clarity, confusion and increasingly, complexity. Too often though, it is ignored, denied or left to chance. That was my experience where there was never any question I would learn anything about sex from my parents. As was typical, I learnt from one of the neighbourhood kids during primary school. Martin was in the same year as me, but a different class. We were sprung in his back yard one day during a pissing competition – see who could get the furthest, do the neatest figure of eight. To us this was little different to spitting water melon seeds, but to Martin's god-bothering parents it was a big deal. It seemed there was shame in taking enjoyment here, even from pissing.

When Martin gave me the low down on sex, he made it sound as though he knew what he was talking about, that he had *always* known, and that somehow I was behind the times because I didn't. The next day I heard that Martin himself had been given sex education only the day before my lesson, by an older brother of one of the kids in the area. Sadly, I didn't find anyone else to educate on these matters.

Sometime after this I went with my parents on a holiday to Port Lincoln, an eight hour drive around the peninsulas of South Australia. Here I got sun burnt, sea sick and, with only a basic understanding of the mechanics involved, had my first sexual awakening.

We stayed in a motel, in two wings with a boiling concrete car park in between. Across the car park was a clear view of other units. In one of these a young girl, a few years older than me, was getting dressed. She wore only underpants and a singlet, with the outline of her breasts evident. With her back to the window she brushed her hair. I was transfixed. And then she bent over.

I'm sure there's nothing unique in this, but as my understanding of, and interest in the mechanics grew, my greatest fear over some long years was that I might die a virgin.

I think most of the girls around the place in my early teenage years had a similar level of sex education. Seemed that nothing was said to many of them until menstruation started. Sex roles were also fixed. There were names for those girls who were known or believed, to do sex, which hasn't changed much in the decades since. Boys had little responsibility. There was a common belief that withdrawal would prevent pregnancy.

I was friendly with Michelle in an odd sort of way. We didn't really hang around together but sometimes walked home from school together. I harboured ambitions but Michelle always seemed a little out of reach, a little too sophisticated for me. Strangely I rarely saw her on weekends, no matter how many times I nonchalantly walked past her house. This was run-down – peeling paint and loose fly screens – with a broken down car permanently in the front yard. I had never been inside nor seen anyone else in the house – parents or siblings.

Then, with no notice, Michelle disappeared, never to return. Pregnant and shipped out I suspect, for that's how things were done in those days. She certainly wasn't the only magically vanished girl.

Almost 50 years later, while visiting Adelaide, I took myself around the streets of Edwardstown where so much had happened in my formative years. I came across Michelle's house, virtually unchanged, still with a broken down car in the front yard, though it was now Commodore not FC.

My first sexual experiences were not elegant and I'm not sure how much pleasure I provided. Too pre-occupied to notice. And what does it say when you can't remember the name of the girl you first had sex with? It would, I think, only be fair if she didn't remember my name, but then again, I wasn't her first.

When an adult engages in sexual behaviour with children under the age of consent (16 in most states, 17 in South Australia and Tasmania) they are committing a criminal offence of child sexual abuse. While there may be degrees of culpability in offences between, say, very young children and those almost at age of consent, or where there are significant power imbalances such as an adult with a level of authority over the child, the law is the law. And Australian law says a person under the age of consent cannot legally consent to sexual contact.

Criminality of sexual activity between adults and children is based on a belief this causes harm to children. This is often described as ruining their lives. While there may often be negative impacts I can't see that this necessarily 'ruins a life' and it's melodramatic to claim so. I appreciate that terrible things happen to some people and this can have major impacts on lives long after, but what's left when there is no hope for better times? What is a person supposed to think about the rest of their life when they are told it's been ruined?

From time to time the media reports on teachers who have sexually abused students. It's absolutely right that teachers and others responsible for the care of children have a duty of care: a moral and legal obligation to ensure their safety and well-being. Clearly there are boundaries and while it's true that different people have different personal boundaries it's difficult for a child to ensure those boundaries are adhered to. And a child may not want to adhere to those boundaries. The law might be black and white, but in practice it's not so clear cut.

Even as a teenager I was never comfortable sharing sexual experiences – real or imagined – with other boys. That isn't to say I didn't do it, just that it didn't feel right. As I grew older I was even less comfortable. So all I'm going to say here is that I'm grateful for the practical sex lessons I received as a sixteen year old from a young woman.

I understand research that indicates young males sexually abused by females can, and do, suffer similar difficulties in later life to those young males abused by older males. And that an early sexual experience with an older woman has the potential to sexualise all relationships with women.

But when is it abuse? In my case I wasn't a virgin, I wasn't manipulated or coerced. This was a time limited and respectful relationship. From the experience I learnt consideration and patience. I have thought deeply on the morality of the experience, and believe it would have been wrong for Carol to have been punished in any way for this.

In Tim Winton's novel *Breath*, set in West Australia, the central character – a fifteen year old boy known as Pikelet – has his first sexual experience with an older woman. Eva is an exotic American in her mid-twenties. The experience is over a prolonged period rather than a one-off. In the book, after one of their encounters, Eva tells Pikelet: 'Don't brag about me, okay? ... not to anyone.'

Reading that was like a thunderbolt, for perhaps forty years earlier, something very similar had been asked of me.

One fine Sunday afternoon a long-standing girlfriend and I were sprung semi-naked in the back seat of a car I had a loan of. This may sound brazen but it was in a well out of the way location, so there was an element of bad luck in the policeman going down the road and deciding to investigate the car on the side of the road. J was nearly 15, I was 16. At the police station my parents were told that I would be charged with Indecent Interference, which sounds awfully dirty-old-manish. Next day back at the police station we were told the charges wouldn't go ahead. At home the incident was not spoken of again. Too embarrassing I'm guessing.

Later on a girlfriend and I split, with a little drama thrown in for no good reason. I managed to find another girlfriend quite quickly and went about this quite happily. Then the first girlfriend wanted to get back. I said no thanks, quite graciously I thought. Her mother called me to explain J was distraught, had expressed suicidal thoughts. I gently stuck to my position.

J had the usual teenage difficulties along with low self-esteem and particularly poor relations with her father. A severely disabled sister caused great angst and public embarrassment with no support or capacity to deal with this.

A few weeks after the phone call from her mother I heard J had been in a gang bang. I have no idea of her emotional state at the time, but a few weeks earlier it had not been good. And I have no idea of her level of control over the experience. But I find it easier to believe she was taken advantage of than I do to believe she was fully enthusiastic throughout. I hope her life has turned out well.

Given the times, and the limited availability of contraception, it was almost inevitable that, later on, another girlfriend became pregnant. We had talked about this, in the way that young adults occasionally have mature conversations on things of some import. N was catholic and did not believe in abortion. I was a-religious at that time. Didn't think much about it but believed in abortion. When it happened there was a reversal. I was prepared for a baby if N wanted, but she decided on a termination and this was her decision. Shortly after we broke up.

I had confided in the branch manager of the bank where I worked, saying N wanted an abortion. 'Don't do it,' he said, offering to find nearby employment for N with accommodation thrown in for us both. 'If you do, you'll spend the rest of your life wondering about the baby.' He was wrong. I don't, though I can't speak for N.

Late one night during a dark and lonely period of my late twenties in Darwin, I called a brothel. Arrangements were made for me to call in to premises on the edge of town, pay the fee and then meet a young lady in the lobby of a hotel in town. This all went as arranged and we went up the stairs to the first floor. She opened the door and I followed her in.

In my situation, wanting sex or perhaps just a fleeting connection, my purchase was rational. Assuming the young woman was providing the service of her own volition, this too was rational. Business, pure and simple.

The room had clearly not long been vacated. The bed was rumpled, damp towels on the floor. An empty beer can on each of the bed side tables. 'Oh! I'm sorry,' she said, and moved towards the bed as if to make it more inviting. 'Sorry,' I said. 'I can't do this.' And left. That may have been the best $100 I ever spent.

There was a time in one of my relationships when I didn't hear the words: 'Not tonight darling'. This was a relationship with an active and satisfying sex life. I started doing what we often did. When I realised there was no reciprocation, that this was not wanted, I immediately stopped. Shame faced in the dark I apologised. She thanked me. Many years later, as I write this, I feel an awkward sensation. Education is a life-long event.

A house built on sand

The following vignettes focus on small incidents that illustrate through specific detail a broader picture of troubled teenage years. Difficulties faced by teenagers are well known, but mine were built on shakier-than-usual foundations of alienation, disengagement and low level confidence. Preparation for life was clearly underdone.

There is action – something happening – with small pieces of reflection in each piece, one of which leads with a poem. These pieces show a progression through time from adolescence to early adulthood and through place, both within Adelaide and then the move to Darwin.

1. Some young people have difficulty forming lasting friendships through regular family relocations. Commonly this was a father moving the family around following work. I managed to experience that difficulty with friendships while staying put.

Mavis had some faint element of snobbery. As I was finishing primary school a new high school was set to open. It was about the same distance away as an older school. Most of the kids I hung around with were going to the new one, which was my preference. Mavis, though, was convinced I would get a better education at the older school. A bit like how some people rate the older established inner-city sandstone universities higher than the newer outer suburban or regional institutes. Despite my protests, and I don't give up easily, Mavis insisted I go to the older school. She prevailed. The chip on my shoulder remembered this.

As the Christmas holidays were coming to an end, I became increasingly worried about the start of high school. Specifically about turning up on my own on the first day. I got wind that a bunch of kids, who were not part of the cohort I had hung around with, were planning to rendezvous and then head off together. Uninvited I turned up at the pre-arranged meeting place. A couple of the kids made it clear I wasn't expected, nor particularly welcome, but would be tolerated on the journey to the unknown.

Arrival at the gates of Marion High School was a little like running the gauntlet. Older kids were lined up to jeer and sneer at the newcomers in an atmosphere of impending violence, which proved to be the case. And Marion wasn't even noted as a tough school.

2. WE WERE NOT CLOSE

 though I knew him well.
 The cheeky grin under the curly mop
 belied the rage within.
 Always on duty.
 Tough as nuts on the footy field,

on prowl in the schoolyard,
always up for a Saturday night fight.
School failed to satisfy.
Rejecting the rules, the discipline,
to everyone's relief he left.
Opted for different rules, discipline.
The navy posted him far away.
News came a little later, of a car crash.
Fleeing the police, it was said.
None were surprised.
This was always to be the fate of That Boy.

Many years later, living in that place,
I sought out the newspaper story.
'Worst scene ever,' the hardened traffic cop had said.
I drove the straight road, past the ditch,
where That Boy died.
And wondered.
Did it have to be inevitable?

Poetry forces a focus on each and every word, demanding removal of the unnecessary. It invites imagery, a subtle rhythm, perhaps a rhyme. It slows the reader and draws attention through its line breaks. I once heard a university academic, in the field of English literature, say they use poetry to focus or crystallise the essence of something they need to write as an academic paper. I have tried to do something similar, as a means of capturing the heart of the matter. Following now is the prose companion to the poem I opened this vignette with.

From quite an early age I was increasingly given more freedom. There was little question over where I was going or who with. And even less verification. As a teenager I learnt how to get around night-time suburban and city streets. I learnt to stay cool under pressure, how to swing things to an advantage, or minimise the disadvantage and I carried this into adulthood.

Dances in suburban halls were quite common. Crossing the dance floor, with all eyes watching, only to be rebuffed by a girl was nearly as bad as the gauntlet that needed to be run on leaving. Here, older groups of teens, with nothing better to do, or an eye for the girls, hung around their cars menacingly.

Later on, parties were a regular feature, whenever someone or other's parents were away. Here, alcohol was common, along with the almost mandatory fight. These were fair fights. When someone had had enough that was it. Putting the boot in would have been unthinkable. I was tall for my age and at these parties there was often enough an older guy, shorter than I was, who wanted to make a name for himself by beating up the big guy. I managed to get by. Surprising really, considering I never learnt to fight. Just wasn't interested in it.

One of the kids I went to school with was a real rough nut, who I have given the name That Boy. He and I weren't close but we played footy together, which creates a bond of sorts. That Boy was always up for a fight. I remember one party quite vividly, he and his opponent slugging it out on the verandah of a federation house, with the rest of the party goers watching on. This went on for some time but didn't pass stalemate. At some point they stopped, realising it was unlikely to be a decisive victory for either, shook hands and wandered off together, chatting amiably.

That Boy had a good heart. I recall him standing up for a little kid being monstered by older kids in the schoolyard. Always seemed to be in trouble with teachers, and left early to join the navy. That was the last heard of him for a few years until news came he had been killed in a car crash, near where he had been stationed at a navy base.

The news came with various embellishments to fit the legend. He had been fleeing from police when the car accident happened. It was a stolen car. He had been absent from the navy without permission and was being sought by naval police. Whatever it was, or wasn't, few were surprised. His death was seen as almost inevitable.

Decades later I lived nearby the place where That Boy died. Feeling a strong urge to know more, I searched out newspaper reports of the accident. 'Worst scene ever,' was the headline.

3. Whereas the Edwardstown house was old, dark and dingy, the Eden Hills house was light and airy. Mavis and Pax had spent countless hours through countless disagreements designing the house and now they took some delight in the view from the lounge room down King William Street, Adelaide city's main thoroughfare. And the city lights. Adelaide people had a thing about the city lights: perhaps because most of them lived on the extensive Adelaide plain. With its increased elevation Eden Hills had a totally different vibe to far more developed Edwardstown.

Grandfather and I at last had something in common: resentment at having to move. He had lived in the Edwardstown house most of his life and although he had been slowing down with age, leaving his shed (and cabinet-making) behind was a wrench. During the first winter at Eden Hills arguments between him and Mavis were a nightly occurrence and became quite fierce. He wanted to keep the strip heater on, alongside his bed. Mavis, convinced he would burn the house down, wanted it turned off once he was in bed. During one of these arguments he fell and broke a hip. Devastating for an old person. As he was taken away to hospital, he claimed she pushed him. She may have, though I can't imagine she intended to cause damage. He died soon after, in hospital.

4. Early one wet winter Saturday night, during my last year of high school, I called on a few of the kids I was hanging around with at that time. There was nothing planned for the night, and no particular prospect of anything like a good night out. One by one they all declined to go out, preferring a dry and warm night at home.

Though still early, with no other options I headed home, hitch-hiking as usual. In school uniform this was easy, out of school uniform, much harder. But on this night I got picked up almost straight away. After being dropped off I walked down the lane from the main road to our house. I stood on the street looking up. It wouldn't have been eight o'clock.

I turned, walked back up the lane to the main road and headed back down the hill to where I had just come from. This time I didn't try and hitch. I didn't have anywhere to go, but I had plenty of time.

5. I got myself suspended from school once, for smoking. The suspension was from lunchtime on a Friday, which was a half-day holiday, until one or other of my parents came to the school. I went home on the Friday afternoon, and not wanting to put a dampener on the weekend, waited until Sunday night to break the news. They were pissed off, but I like to think there may have been a small glimmer in Pax's eye.

Wagging school was a common enough occurrence. On one of these days a couple of us went in to Adelaide for a Vietnam moratorium march. In Adelaide these drew much smaller crowds than the bigger cities and we spent most of our time avoiding television cameras, making sure we didn't end up on the evening news.

There were different ways of dealing with these absences, but I reckoned I had it perfected. Each week teachers and parents were expected to sign a student diary. It was in here that absences were noted. For a couple of years, supported by my skills of forgery, I ran a couple of diaries. One for the teachers, one for the parents. Genius.

6. During high school years I often worked a variety of jobs through the school holidays. Unloading toilets off a truck once, delivering furniture several times, stacking supermarket shelves, serving hot dogs and chips at a fast food stall at the Adelaide Show for a couple of days – not my forte. I hated it. On arrival for the morning of the third day I told the boss I was quitting. 'You got in first,' he said. 'I was going to quit you,' as he handed over the pay envelope he had already prepared in readiness for my departure. And then he shook my hand, which was a remarkably generous thing to do.

One of my holiday jobs was general hand at my brother-in-law's public relations business. Pax used to say he had champagne tastes on a beer budget. Loved a flash car, and the high life. Happy enough to hire me for holiday work, but he forgot to pay me.

Out on the town one Saturday night I saw him walking along, arm around … not my sister. We came close and looked directly at each other, but didn't speak.

Sunday afternoon visits from my sister and he were regular events. Late next afternoon as I was arriving home, walking up the driveway, he looked through the window at me and raised a finger to his lips.

When the chance arose, alone outside at the barbeque, he explained the young woman had some problems and he was helping her deal with them. Which is, I have long since suspected, what they all say. No clarification was sought on my part, but I reminded him he owed me. He promptly paid up. My moral compass was in its infancy.

Adolescent behaviour is often inconsistent with beliefs about right and wrong and heavily susceptible to influence by peers and role models. Dealing tactfully with difficult situations was not something I had grown up with. In retrospect I'm not sure what I might have done: whether I could, or should, have bought my sister up to date. I was 16 and didn't have the skills to solve that dilemma, but at the time I was happy enough to get paid.

Tense is generally past for life story or memoir, as in, 'I was a difficult child,' or, 'I reminded him he owed me.' But if memoir writing is about character development, about how the writer has changed over time or due to experience, then there is a place for the present tense, as in 'I am now able to see how circumstances shaped me,' or, 'I'm not sure what I might have done.'

7. Once I started high school either Mavis or Pax would occasionally talk about the importance of a career. As a wilful youth I would ask why they wanted to talk about that place over near China.

I don't recall ever being excited by school, ever having a feeling of enjoying learning something, or being delighted by an interest shown in me by any teacher. During one holiday period while working at Woolworths, a couple of university students came in and spoke with the younger staff. Two young women, not much older than me, were doing a survey as part of their course in one of the social sciences. 'What ambition do you have?' is the one question I recall. 'Nothing really,' I answered, before walking away. Angry at their questions, angry at my answer. Angry at them because they had answers to their questions.

In South Australia at that time there were seven years of primary schooling, followed by five secondary years. I failed year four at high school. Could have gone on to a fifth year but this would have been doing internal subjects. That would not have allowed me to go to university should I have wanted to. I chose to repeat the year, tried no harder but did much better.

After five dismal years, but prior to the matriculation year, I left school with little idea of what I wanted to do. All I knew, with total clarity, was that I did not want to work in a factory. There were many of these nearby and it was a common enough aspiration among my cohort to get a job in one, but the noise, the smell, assaulted my senses. I wasn't interested in a trade or the defence forces. Options were limited and from that perspective it could be seen that the administrative classes were my best, if not only, avenue into the workforce.

And so it was that in early January 1973, Mavis roused me out of bed, instructed me to put the suit on she had bought me, and go to town and get a job. Which is what I did. Head office of the Commercial Bank of Australia was about the fourth door I entered where I satisfactorily passed their selection hoops and was offered a job, to start at a branch near home in about a month. That was how easy it was in 1973. 'And get a haircut before you start,' was the final instruction delivered as I was on the way out the door. 'Just before you start.'

Dismal, about to meet the new dismal.

8. At 18 I moved out of home, which Mavis and Pax felt reflected badly on them and caused a great deal of upset. A year or so later, after an ever-changing cast of house-mates, with struggling resources and incompetence at managing most aspects of life, I moved back. This was a disaster. In retrospect – my great sage in the sky – I should have foreseen this and got my act together. My incompetence may have had something to do with the amount of time I spent inside pubs, though I have had some valuable lessons there.

One time in Adelaide, shortly after becoming a legal drinker, I was talking with an older guy, a witty and popular regular, who younger guys like me were happy to be seen talking to. He mentioned he had just started holidays. 'Are you going somewhere?' I asked. 'Naaah,' he replied. 'If I go somewhere I'll just sit in a pub so I may as well stay here.' I liked a drink, too much perhaps, but thought there had to be more to life than that.

Another time, same pub late on a Saturday afternoon, the barman called me over as I entered. 'You're a good lad,' he said, or words to that effect. 'But I'm never serving you rum again.' I have no recollection of what I may have done the night before, but this was good advice. Well received, well heeded. I've barely drunk it, or any spirits since, beer and wine being my preferred poison.

Looking back years later, this barman along with a football coach, may well have been the only adults I paid any heed to. Role models were in short supply.

At 20 I accepted the transfer to Darwin. This was a revelation after white bread Adelaide. Multicultural before the term was in common use, I discovered food beyond meat and three veg and started to learn something of Aboriginal Australia. I also created some opportunities, and learnt something about myself.

Crime wave

I have tales to tell of my teenage crime, which spanned a few years. I am bookending and contextualising these tales within a sociological lens, as I wrote about in the first part of this book. This allows me to open with a professional experience (well after the teenage years) and close with a strongly held view on the injustice commonly seen in government policy. The tales of my personal experience, which provide the middle section, are told in several discrete short pieces which could each stand alone and be thought of as flash nonfiction. The personal essay though, is a form that allows a deeper exploration of events and situations. Overlaying the global context on the personal situation adds depth and universality.

For a few years from 2016 I worked on a casual basis as a convenor of Youth Justice Conferences. These are forums that bring together a young offender (12-17 years of age) who has admitted their guilt or been found guilty, along with the victim, a police officer and various support people. The conference is a form of restorative justice.

Restorative justice sees crime as an act against individuals and the community, whereas traditional retributive justice sees crime as an act against the state and its laws. In restorative justice accountability comes through taking responsibility and restoring harm. Retributive justice allocates accountability through punishment. This is a deficit model where the crime defines the offender. Restorative justice, where the offender takes responsibility and repairs the harm, is an asset model.

It aims to help the young person realise the impact they have had on others and take some steps to make things right and get a better connection with their community. The approach is based on a belief that the less time the young person spends in the justice system the better the long-term outcome. And there is enormous power in the offender and the victim being in the same room, speaking together.

There is a common belief that youth justice conferences are a soft touch and the kid is getting off lightly. Too lightly. I particularly enjoyed those conferences where the victim starts the process with this belief, not wanting to waste their time. 'Put your pre-conceptions aside,' I would say, 'and give it a try. The kid will probably learn more hearing from you than they will in hearing from a magistrate.' Sometimes I would get a feeling the kid wasn't going to learn from the experience and would be likely to continue on their way. But more often than not I sensed this was going to work.

A 13-year old boy had spray painted a local business premise, including the security camera that made his identification simple. Not overly bright, you'd have to say, but 13-year olds aren't always noted for forward thinking. There had been a couple of previous police cautions for shoplifting and he was clearly on a downward trajectory. Getting to know him, just a little, I discovered a shy but thoughtful young fellow. It came out that his mother was drug addicted and homeless. His father had brain damage and couldn't cope with the stress of the conference. Presumably he had trouble coping with other daily stresses of life. I discovered this 13-year old cared deeply about his father and provided a high level of support for him. In the conference connections were made with community services where the boy could get involved in different activities. And was genuinely keen to do so. And where support could be provided to help him cope with his father's condition. That conference, I feel certain, turned things around for the better. The victim agreed.

During the interview for the position of conference convenor I was asked to demonstrate my understanding and or experience of youth development, community programs and restorative justice. I wasn't asked about my personal experience of youth crime, but had I been, I may have rated quite highly.

One weekend when I was about 14 my parents were away, leaving me at home with my grandfather. Late on the Friday afternoon a couple of plain clothes police pulled into the driveway. One of them showed me a card, which I presume was some sort of identification, but I didn't ask for a close inspection. They said they were there because of reports of stolen milk money in the area. And I had been accused. Guilty of stealing milk money I was, but I had not done this for at least a few weeks. Honest.

They came into the house and my bedroom where they quickly noticed the money my mother had left for the weekend. About two dollars in ten and twenty cent coins. In their eyes this was proof positive of my guilt. On hearing my explanation one of them said he didn't believe me. And that they would be back after my parents returned.

As they were leaving my grandfather, who I was not close to, went and spoke with them. He then came to me and, quite distraught, said he didn't believe I had done it. I didn't understand why he was so upset. Decades later I discovered his son, my uncle Gordon for whom I am named – Graeme Gordon Gibson – had a criminal history. And I now understand the source of grandfather's distress: first his son, then his grandson.

I didn't mention the matter of the police visit with my parents on their return and I imagine grandfather must have found it too difficult to bring it up with them, for the matter was never raised. This was a family with a knack for avoiding the difficult. And those plain clothes police never came back.

As an 18 year old in 1929, Uncle Gordon had stolen membership money from the local Masonic club, of which his father, my grandfather, was treasurer. It's not clear from the newspaper report how criminal charges came to be laid, but the report says grandfather didn't want him sent to gaol and was prepared to take him back. The magistrate told him he: '… should make every effort to go straight,' and released him under the Offenders' Probation Act, with a bond of twenty pounds to be called up for any other offence within two years. Seems Uncle Gordon didn't go terribly straight, as in 1936 he was convicted of stealing money from an employer, and sentenced to three months in prison.

Uncle Gordon's first reported brush with the law had been in 1926, when the 15 year-old was fined seven shillings and sixpence, for riding his bicycle on South Road Edwardstown at night without lights. I don't know whether the South Australian police have a vendetta against bicycle riding teenage boys from the Gibson family of Edwardstown, but I distinctly recall being harassed by the police while riding a bicycle. On South Road Edwardstown.

Uncle Gordon died a couple of years before I was born, and I don't recall him ever being spoken of. Just like a country, a family can have a selective memory of its history.

Curiously, half a century later on the other side of the country, I became friends with the milkman's daughter. Cath had often helped with the milk run and recalled the spate of missing milk money. She graciously accepted my apology, but the decent thing would have been for me to offer a few dollars as partial recompense. In ten and twenty cent coins.

When I was 15 a group of kids I was hanging around with joined a boy's youth club at a local church. They ran activities on a Friday night which we went to sometimes. Nothing much interesting ever happened. My parents weren't too interested in what I was doing but hearing I was off to the church youth club must have been satisfying.

One night we broke into the hall alongside the church with the intention of helping ourselves to a bottle of wine someone had seen. It wasn't to be found, so we left. No damage was done, the window was even shut behind us as we left. But we were noticed. The police came and for a lengthy period we crawled along the side of the train line as a police car cruised slowly up and down with its spotlight on the track. We kept our nerve and after the police car left waited a good period before making our way off the train line corridor. This was a time when white jeans were all the rage. Mine were absolutely blackened, but it didn't raise a question from Mavis when she did the laundry.

One long weekend the church organised a camp in the Adelaide Hills. A few of us caught a train up on Saturday and back on Monday. On the Saturday night we celebrated by getting horribly drunk on cheap sherry and port. I woke on the Sunday morning, wrapped in blankets alongside a fire. It was winter and wet. I'd been found by one of the church leaders late the night before, asleep in the garden, in the rain. Luckily this fellow was a doctor. My temperature, he told me, had dropped alarmingly and had I stayed out all night – which would have been possible if he hadn't come across me – things would likely have been very different.

On arrival back at Adelaide train station around midday on the Monday, Pax surprised me by being there to greet and take me home. On the way, after a little small talk, which neither of us were good at, he asked what I had been doing the previous weekend. Which meant he had some idea of what I had been doing.

On the Saturday night of that weekend a group of us had a night out with a local lad, a couple of years older than us, with a job and a car. He was quite peculiar, but because he had a car we were forgiving. Never thought to wonder why a 17-year-old with a job and a car would want to cart around a bunch of 15-year-old school kids. We cruised the streets, he bought some alcohol, we took ourselves into the local drive-in theatre through a hole in the back fence and shortly before calling it a night decided to drop into the local laundromat. Nothing much else was open.

The laundromat had a sliding soft drink machine, with bottles standing upright in rows. Upon payment a mechanism was released allowing a bottle to be lifted out. One of the geniuses in our gang had the idea to help ourselves to a drink by using a belt buckle to lift the lid, with a straw from the floor.

We were just leaving when a security guard pulled up, asked what we were doing. 'Looking for my mother,' someone said, 'I was supposed to meet her here.' As we were leaving one kid sat on the boot of the FB Holden to hide the number plate. But the security guard had taken note. He reported us to the police, who took a week before calling on my parents, while I was enjoying a wholesome weekend at the church youth club camp.

Arrangements were made for me to visit the police station with my parents. Here I was told we were to be charged with the larceny of the contents of three bottles of soft drink. While at the police station I was asked to leave the room while the officer spoke to my parents. I overheard him say they wanted us to go to court to give us a fright and get back on the straight and narrow.

It was a long day in court where we were found guilty without conviction. Penalty was a ten dollar fine with loss of licence for three months: after we were old enough to have a licence that was. The lad with the car lost his licence for three months. Which I think was pretty harsh. He lived quite a way from his job.

All of the kids, except the car owner, had a mother in attendance. Mine was deeply distressed by this experience. I recall, in particular, her concern at what the neighbours would say if our case made it into the newspaper. Keeping the family's dirty washing out of public view was an obsession. 'No-one's business but ours,' she would say. The next day one of the other kids told me that his mother had said she wouldn't go shopping with my mother.

I'm not sure whether it was real. I had only ever seen them on TV, but it was heavy on the dashboard of the '67 Holden.

One particular Friday night, while playing a game in the billiards hall – and yes, high-brow though it may seem, billiards was the game of choice – a group of us hatched a plan to raise some cash. Right next door to the billiard hall was the back yard of a corner store, where crate upon crate of empty soft drink bottles were kept after being returned for a cash refund of 10 cents each. South Australia has long been a progressive state and was an early adopter in container deposit legislation.

A couple of us went over the loose barbed wire fence and passed through as many as we could manage to carry between the four of us. Six each, I think. Next step in the heist was to wander down to the nearest shop that refunded empty bottles and cash in. This was at Chris's Fish Shop.

Being incautious types (read: daring, greedy, stupid) we went back to the rear of the corner store and repeated the whole exercise. Two more times. Not an eye-lid was raised at Chris's. Seen stranger things.

As we were leaving the corner store the third time the owner of the billiard hall came out, looked directly at us, but didn't say a word before scuttling back inside. We decided enough was enough and went off on some other mission.

Later that night, as our group had split, going home in different directions, I was walking down the main street almost opposite the corner store, when two figures appeared at the entrance: the shop owner and the owner of the billiard hall. Seeing them before they saw me, I turned and walked quickly away.

As a shouted 'Oi' rang out, I bolted down the road and around the corner. Hadn't gotten far when the '67 Holden pulled up just ahead of me. The driver, owner of the corner store himself, leaned across the front seat and pointed it at me. A revolver.

Following his quietly spoken instructions I got in, at which point he put the revolver on the metal dashboard. Clunk. There was no ranting, raving, just some questions. Why? Where would this sort of behaviour lead? Did I really want a life of crime?

He made a deal with me. We would go back to Chris' Fish Shop and with the little money I had left I would buy empty soft drink bottles. I would then return them to the yard at the back of his shop. The workers at Chris' remained inscrutable: still not raising an eyelid. Surely they hadn't seen this before? A couple of customers, though, thought it a hoot.

I've come to appreciate the wisdom of the shop owner – whose name I wish I remembered – and his ability as a natural educator. But did he really need the revolver? He must have known how dangerous those things could be.

With the advantage of perspective gained from more than a few decades, and an interested life, with a foundation of scepticism and possibility, I can look on those events and ponder what it all meant, why it happened. And how similar acts of incivility or petty crime might impact the lives of other young people.

My juvenile crime spree – which was more extensive than I have outlined here, but you get the picture – was not driven by any need, other than the need for an aimless and disinterested life devoid of adult guidance or role models to fit in with a cohort. It petered out soon after the last escapade I detailed, of its own accord, though largely aided by the enforced move to a new suburb which led to new friendships. I have long since realised this move was possibly the best thing that could have happened, as it got me out of a deteriorating situation which was likely only going to get worse. Many of the kids I moved on from continued the same trajectory and a couple did gaol time after attaining adulthood.

Whether I would have followed on that path is one of the great unknowns of my life, but it is well known that entering the justice system, and prison in particular, is a strong indicator of continuing engagement with that system.

Treating symptoms of a societal problem, such as crime, is easier than addressing underlying causes of crime, such as poverty, mental health concerns or addictions. And then there is the national shame of Indigenous incarceration rates.

I opened this piece talking about youth justice conferences. The reality is that most participants in these are Indigenous. That is no surprise when you consider Indigenous 10 to 17 year olds, who make up around five per cent of that age range, make up around half of all youth in detention in Australia. In the Northern Territory that figure is often up to 100 per cent. Adult incarceration rates are similarly many times higher for Indigenous people.

The full range of socio-economic conditions need to be taken into account when considering this, including the impact of colonialism, dispossession and inter-generational trauma from forced child removals. The *Uluru Statement from the Heart* is an Indigenous consensus position on Indigenous constitutional recognition developed through a national process of regional dialogues and a constitutional convention of 250 Aboriginal and Torres Strait Islander delegates in 2017. Quite a piece of poetry in its own right, its 420 words are fully deserving of attention. It has this to say about incarceration;

> Proportionally, we are the most incarcerated people on the planet. We are not an innately criminal people. Our children are alienated from their families at unprecedented rates. This cannot be because we have no love for them. And our youth languish in detention in obscene numbers. They should be our hope for the future.

With little progress on the justice front you could look at the economics. Locking people up is expensive business. The cost per day is around $200 for an adult and more than six times that for a juvenile. And it doesn't work. The old saying is that prison just turns inmates into better criminals. More than 60 per cent of young people released from detention re-offend within 12 months.

An alternative approach, known as justice reinvestment, involves redirecting money from prisons to front end support services that address the causes of offending. This supports economic efficiency and social justice. In the remote north-west New South Wales town of Bourke where this approach was implemented in 2013, offending rates and recidivism are down and social outcomes have improved. It seems only blind ideology has prevented this approach being more widely adopted.

I can understand self-interested privately operated prisons, enjoying seemingly endless years of growth, not being over-enthused by a different approach. But the fact it has taken until a change of federal government in 2022 to offer greater support for what is clearly in the public interest is beyond disappointing.

And I recognise the major challenge of explaining and gaining understanding of complex issues among the general public, many of whom don't have the time, willingness or capacity to engage, preferring tried and trusted home spun solutions and hand-me-down wisdoms. That difficulty is exacerbated by politicians who seek to whip up community concerns with promises of a tough approach, ignoring inconvenient evidence and sensible alternatives. So predictable has this become that Law and Order has segued into the meme, Laura Norder, with whom I have had more than one close encounter. And you never know when Laura Norder will show up.

My load of garden waste and I were turned away from the local dump the other day. The office had been burgled overnight and the police were investigating. On its re-opening the next day I got talking to the bloke next to me, while off-loading. As you do.

An amiable bloke, he'd been busy in his elderly neighbour's garden. Helping others was part of his make-up, what he enjoyed doing in his retirement. Like me, he too had been turned away the previous day, but he'd travelled much further than I. 'Bloody nuisance too,' he said.

The conversation then went something close to this;

'Lot of crime around lately. More and more of it. There was a whole lot of cars broken into the other week. And a lady I know, old lady, had her bag stolen walking along the street. The mongrels pushed her to the ground.'

'That's pretty awful,' I contributed, feeling I knew where this was leading.

'Sentencing's too light, that's the problem,' he added with certainty, confirming I knew where this was leading.

'Instead of giving 'em one year they should give 'em ten. That'd soon get the message out.'

I pondered his response for a moment, then ventured, 'Trouble with that is that people who go to jail generally come out better crooks than they were when they went in.'

'Well I suppose that's true enough,' he responded reasonably, creased brow suggesting I had discombobulated the simple certainty of his crime-busting solution.

I've worked in adult learning a long time, with a special interest in informal learning and a deep belief that people learn best what they learn for themselves. Being lectured to runs a distant last so I left it at that, to let it sink in a little more, waiting to see if he would return to the subject. If so, I thought I'd throw in something about the cost of locking people up.

Then another ute pulled up on the other side of my new friend, who greeted the new arrival. Unsurprisingly their conversation started with the inconvenience of the dump being closed the day before. Then, a re-run.

'More and more crime around lately,' from my new friend. 'Lot of cars were broken into the other day.' I shamelessly eavesdropped, pulling branches off one at a time to keep the noise down so I could hear where this went. 'And some mongrels pushed an old lady I know to the ground when she had her bag stolen.'

What next? Was my new friend about to remain faithful to his solution of 'lock 'em up and throw away the key'? Or had I sowed a seed of doubt, introducing some level of nuance to his thinking? By now I looked like I was on a go-slow work rule, so keen was I to hear where the conversation was going.

And just then a four wheel drive rumbled in next to me and I didn't hear another word. Bugger.

Endurance

The following vignettes provides specific detail of vivid memories. Writing in the present tense brings a sense of immediacy and sharpens the focus, which was my aim with the 100 words that comprise the first vignette. Sometimes you can say a lot in a little. The sparse use of dialogue highlights the sadness in the first vignette, the irreverence in the second. The third and fourth vignettes are my best reflections on two lives as they were lived.

1. I am 16. It is late at night, or perhaps very early morning. Mavis is in the kitchen smoking, listening to the radio, doing a crossword or studying the form guide and keeping track of her winnings. On more than one of these nights Pax comes to the kitchen with a poignant plea: 'Come to bed.' Mavis responds with: 'I will in a minute,' or, 'Just finishing this.'

I do not know whether this was Pax's desire for intimacy with his wife. Or just his sense that this wasn't right, wasn't normal behaviour and something was wrong. Which it was.

2. 'Well that's one way of getting rid of the bastards,' was Mavis's succinct view when Australia's Liberal Prime Minister Harold Holt disappeared. I was 12 and not much into politics, but guessed Mr Holt and his mob were not favoured in our house.

The 17th December 1967 was the day Holt went for the swim that needed no towel, never to be seen again after entering very rough water near Melbourne. Various conspiracy theories soon surfaced, some combined with rumours about Holt's personal life. It was suicide, or he faked his death. The CIA were involved, or he was collected and whisked away by a Chinese submarine. He had swum around to the next bay, and then joined a lover in the south of France, is one of the best.

Holt has entered the Australian lexicon, with to 'do a Harold Holt,' referring to any disappearing act. In 1988 a rugby league commentator, lamenting one team's inability to win a premiership, said: 'Waiting for Cronulla to win a Grand Final is like leaving a porch light on for Harold Holt.'

Just five years later, in December 1972, Mavis's political allegiances had changed. I was still short of voting age by a few months but I was taking an interest now. Labor's Don Dunstan had been premier of South Australia for a couple of years, bringing a range of social and cultural changes along with a flamboyant style. Gough Whitlam was expected to win the federal election for the Australian Labor Party. He had something interesting to say and things looked exciting. Mavis, though, was up in arms about the socialist agenda.

What had changed I did not know, but thinking back on it, Pax's career trajectory had taken off about then, with a company car and presumably a pay rise. Which may have meant a higher tax bracket. Self-interest perhaps.

While writing this I listened to a radio discussion about issues people of different political views have while trying to sustain long-term relationships. Food for thought. Before Mavis's switch I suspect she and Pax were very much aligned politically. Political discussion between the like-minded are generally genial. Or rambunctiously agreeable.

Mavis was an avid consumer of news, or opinion masquerading as news on talk-back radio. This was a font of knowledge, a source of inspiration, a proxy life-coach. She saw the world in black and white and always knew what was right. And with a broad generosity she was always ready to share her views, unstoppable on occasion. Pax's response, as I observed it, was one of disciplined silence. 'Let it go, don't take the bait,' I imagine he told himself.

I don't know how suddenly the change in Mavis's allegiances came about. And I can't begin to imagine how she and Pax managed her changing views. Civil conversation and genuine exploration seem unlikely.

Pax held his Labor allegiance closer and longer. As he was dying in early 1992, with Australia in a high unemployment, high interest rate recession, he told me, with a touch of sadness I thought: 'It might be time to give the other mob a go.'

3. For as long as I can remember Mavis and Pax had a plan to visit England when Pax retired. Mavis, a monarchist with a corgi and, she liked to think, a passing resemblance to the Queen, wanted to see the changing of the guard at Buckingham Palace. Pax, a cricket tragic, wanted to see a test match at Lords.

On Pax's retirement from his position at Repco he was offered a job in Darwin for a year, where I was living at the time. Pax had been in Darwin during the war and had visited many times with his work. He had a fondness for the place. It couldn't be said that we became close, but it was during this time my relationship with my parents may have peaked. I was an adult after all.

Mavis's only travels out of South Australia had, up till then, been to Melbourne and Darwin was a major adventure. It might have been enough adventure. On their return to Adelaide after a year they dropped the England travel plans. They may have come to the conclusion it would require more time together than would be comfortable for both of them. Mavis continued her routine of talk back radio and following the horses. Pax had his escape at golf and the Masonic Lodge, with committee work for both to keep him occupied.

Perhaps life's disappointments stacked up. Pax drank more in his later years than had been the case earlier. Friendships contracted. Few attended Pax's funeral in 1992. None at Mavis's funeral ten years later.

4. Mavis and Pax were married for 50 years until Pax's death in 1992. I have few memories of them being happy or showing any signs of

being satisfied for anything other than brief periods. But perhaps many long-term marriages are like this, little more than convenience, or habit. I doubt either of them even thought about ending their marriage, or living apart, and I cannot imagine them ever discussing it. I have never felt I knew them well – and I have thought on this a lot – but I knew them well enough to believe a discussion of that magnitude was out of their orbit. Stoicism was their bedrock.

Perhaps though, because I didn't know them intimately, I have lived my life unaware of their feelings. Perhaps they were satisfied with their lives and their marriage. This may have been controlled by low expectations, but how could I know? Dreams and ambitions were not part of the family conversation, such as that was.

There is no doubt I was loved as a child, but I don't recall ever hearing it. And there was never any doubt about my being cared for in the physical sense. Always clothed, fed and provided with all the essentials and many of the non-essentials, though it was an indifferent upbringing. Benign neglect is how I think of it.

Dysfunction was the default. Whenever a problem arose it was generally ignored or given lip service. Effective communication, problem solving and anger management were not practiced. Occasionally a voice was raised or a door slammed. I contributed my fair share of that.

I don't mean to belittle my parents, and I have thought extensively on how to bring them into this story. They did what they could with the means they had. They were a product of their own upbringing, of which I know little. My two siblings and I all entered short and unhappy marriages. Speaking for myself, which is all I can do here, this was on the cards from the outset. At the end of their lives they left three adult children who individually and independently decided their optimum future did not include the others.

We are a product of our upbringing it is said, but it is also well known that with conscious effort it is possible to grow past that upbringing. I am proof of this, though it took time.

Memory

All memories are fallible, so all you can do is do your best to tell the truth of the memory. You will know when you are leaving out important parts of the story, or misleading. Or lying.

Within the sphere of memoir writing there are masses of memory prompts to help start, guide or refine your writing. For this book I have drawn sketches of the Edwardstown and Eden Hills houses, recalled first memories, looked at what happened on the day of my birth (a United States nuclear test in Nevada) and taken a peek at what the Australian Women's Weekly were focused on in that week's edition: 'HOLLYWOOD'S LOVELIEST WOMEN,' it turns out. None of these proved useful to my writing.

Naming personal character traits is another prompt which I did find useful. It's an exercise in straight if stilted story-telling, that shows the particular trait in action in a short paragraph. This is not a 'king dies, queen dies, kingdom collapses' moment, but it presents something unique about my parents, about their lives and about their impact on me. It also draws a line under their contribution to this book.

Pax

Contributor; Pax had a strong ethic of community service. While I was at primary school, just down the road from our house in Edwardstown, he had been active in the P&C and school sports. Years later it occurred to me that this was how I was chosen in a district representative football team to travel to Perth. My talent wasn't up to it; nepotism was needed. When I started high school, Pax took no further interest in any school or sports activities. He may have felt he had done enough and wanted time for golf, which was a growing passion. Fair enough. Pax was also heavily involved in the Masonic Lodge and Blackwood Golf Club, where he always had committee roles.

Proud; 'A big fish in a small pond,' was how he described himself when knocking back an opportunity for a job in Melbourne. Starting his working life as a welder, over many different jobs, he rose to the position of state manager for a division of Repco. He took the offer of a job in Darwin on retirement as an endorsement of his abilities.

Gentle; It is not uncommon for people to be better grandparents than they were parents and Pax loved his Adelaide grandchildren. Softly spoken and considered in his opinions he was thoughtful to others. Mostly. During a primary school sports carnival Pax was helping cook the sausages while the kids lined up. One enterprising kid, a local I suspect but definitely not from our school, thought he'd try his chances. As he reached the head of the queue Pax recognised an interloper. 'Go on get out,' he said, with a flourish of the tongs, and a tone far sharper than needed. 'You're not one of ours.' He may have been trying to impress the other barbeque dads, but I was saddened by this.

Cruel; Mavis and he had a lengthy but difficult relationship with limited capacity to empathise with each other. Mavis's attitudes and responses were often met with mental cruelty. He could and did, put her down, often in front of others.

Sad; Pax was diagnosed with cancer at about the time of his 50th wedding anniversary. He lasted nine months and died a miserable death, unable, it seemed to me, to accept the inevitability. During my last visit to Adelaide, before he went in to palliative care, he spent most of the time in a darkened bedroom. We had never been particularly close and closeness didn't come during this time. He cried when I said goodbye, about to return to Brisbane, a week or so before the end. I needed to reach out to him at this time and wish I had. I failed him and I failed me.

Mavis

Angry; Mavis started her married life caring for an ailing and largely bed-ridden mother-in-law. She ended her married life caring for a dying husband. I have an enduring image of her cleaning up after Pax's ill-timed visit to the toilet, suffering as he did, from the effects of chemo. All the while muttering to herself. It was at this time, with Pax in a weakened state, that she seized the opportunity to dominate and dominate she did, ruling the roost as never before. Later, with Pax gone, she started a war with the neighbours, and seemingly drove away any remaining friends.

Stubborn; After Pax died, she refused any suggestion of moving to something smaller or more manageable than the Eden Hills house on a steep slope. A retirement village was not countenanced, I think at least partly because she would have had too many other people around her. One day she fell over at the bottom of the driveway and was unable to get up. This was early in the day and someone found her, helping her to her feet and back into the house. 'If that had happened late in the day, or at the top of the driveway you might have been there all night,' I said. 'I don't care,' she replied with clarity and finality. 'If that happens then that happens. I'm not moving.' Ultimately, the decision to stay or go was taken from her. She died in a secure nursing home, with a daily dose of happy pills making her much more docile.

Opinionated; British philosopher Bertrand Russell once said: 'The trouble with the world is that the stupid are cocksure and the intelligent are full of doubt.' Mavis saw the world in black and white and was never shy to offer her views, particularly on current affairs. She was often irrational. I used to explain this by saying she had been dropped on her head as a baby.

Non-conformist; Personal appearance was of little importance to Mavis. Particularly in her later years, she dressed badly. She broke a denture once and, despite Pax's protests, or perhaps because of them, she took weeks to get it fixed. Home duties did not figure highly. Attention to neatness, even cleanliness occupied little of Mavis' time.

Surprising; 'Your father didn't mean what he said. He was just upset.' This was by phone the day after I had called on them in Eden Hills with the news that my marriage was over. Pax's words, before he left the room? 'I thought one of you would have lasted,' referring to his three children, now all with failed marriages. Some years later, during another phone conversation, she told me she loved me.

I have observed and experienced the highs and the lows of personal relationships and have some understanding of their complexity. I see connections between things, how the past can catch up, how one thing leads to another, to another, and often it's quickly downhill.

Some memories won't leave me. A few disparate incidents over a number of years come to mind more often than I think they should. A short story I read had a profound impact, forcing me to think on my experience. These are memories and thoughts are presented here in vignette and flash nonfiction. Observing people living lives of struggle and desperation lead to a poem.

1. 'There's a lot of women living quite remotely up the valleys and creeks out of town,' someone said at a domestic violence forum a year or so back, 'and there's a lot of guns up there.'

   'That's right. I was one of those women a few years back,' someone else said. 'Crawling around behind the trees while my partner, off his face on ice one night, roamed around the block with his shotgun. Looking for me.'

Domestic violence is a fact of life throughout the world and most of it is against women and children. It includes not just physical abuse but emotional, psychological and financial abuse. Being told continuously that you are useless, being cut off from family and friends and having tightly controlled access to money are all insidious, all dangerous. And they all happen.

The council area for the small New South Wales country town I live in, ranks very highly for rates of domestic violence. This is accompanied by other poor socio-economic indicators, like high unemployment levels, limited access to housing, low income levels. On a scale of one to ten, where one is most disadvantaged, we rate a two.

These are difficult topics to discuss in any small town, and my small, friendly town, as the locals like to see it, is no different. And, as in many places, people struggle to identify with the non-physical aspects of domestic violence. As for the physical, 'why doesn't she just leave?' would be a common response.

Committed community support agencies are stretched, working with limited resources and generally short-term government funding. Band-Aids for ruptures is the prescription. For victims, recovery is possible, though to what level is another matter.

> There was a lot of violence in my first marriage. I've gotten over it, I don't dwell on it. But there's one thing I can't forget. A frying pan really does go "boing" when it hits you on the head. Just like the cartoons.
>
> **Life writing workshop participant**

At a fairly minor level – and yes, that is my subjective view – I have form. I don't beat myself up on this but I think about it from time to time. Some things are worth thinking on.

2. I understand women are more likely than men to initiate divorce. In a perfect world the levels of initiation might be more equal, but in our society women are, in many aspects, not equal. I, as a male, have had a life-time's freedom to walk down the road, gazing about, seeking eye contact if I wish. With men and women. Freedom like that is not a given for women. That's a very basic, very stark difference.

Initiating a divorce includes some level of mental preparedness, possibly envisioning different responses. And hopefully some careful planning, as any new venture should.

I also understand divorce is often harder for men and that many men may not grieve in a healing way. If they allow themselves to grieve at all. There is a loss of identity, a loss of certainty, of control over their life. It may not have been their idea. In my case it wasn't, though I quickly came to see it as a good idea, even if the implementation wasn't what I may have liked.

Physical and mental health can suffer as resentment and anger rise with little respite. Coercive and controlling behaviour by men are the greatest indicators of the likelihood of murder of women. The number of women killed by a partner or former partner in Australia is a national disgrace.

In the mid 1980s, I worked casually in a local pub in western Sydney. The sort of pub with a stool in the corner reserved for a regular. Where an ensemble of old blokes would wile away the day over a few schooners. An occasional flurry on the pokies when the TV lost its attraction. The sort of pub where the manager would take an empty Jim Beam bottle down to the cellar and refill it with Australian bourbon. Good for the bottom line.

During a quiet afternoon shift I found myself alone for some time with one of the regulars, Barry. A big bear of a man in his early 50s, rolled his own, drank Tooheys New and worked for the railways. Normally loud but with no-one else around Barry didn't need to shout. Quite softly he confided in me how unhappy he had been since his wife had left. How rarely he saw the kids.

Over the course of the afternoon, as he drank more and as the regulars rolled in, he got louder and he unloaded. 'What a bitch. Took me for everything and then pissed off.' That sort of thing. I was a little sympathetic at the start, becoming less interested in Barry and his sad life as the shift went on. Then, the stunner. His wife, it came out, had not left quite recently as I had imagined, but eight years earlier. Eight years and this bloke had not come to terms with it. All that pent-up anger and rage, making real the metaphor of a walking time bomb. Back then there were plenty like Barry. Still are.

3. I think sometimes of a close acquaintance from some years ago. Not quite a friend but someone I knew well enough. Her daughter, in the rebellious teenage years caused much grief and self-harm. Keen to help her daughter find a way through life, she supported her on an organised cattle trek through outback Queensland, moving slowly each day, camping out at night.

At one point a group of young men from a nearby station came out in the late afternoon. Sat around the campfire, rolled out their swags then up early and off to work next morning. They returned nightly. My close acquaintance's daughter found something she had longed for in one of these young men. After a period as the trek moved on and it became too far to travel back each day he offered a deal. Come stay with me, he said. She didn't have to think too hard.

A few years later with a couple of kids and another on the way, on a remote station far from town, her world had changed. Any semblance of control over her life, gone. My close acquaintance plotted to get her daughter out, away from the Bundy drinking dream gone sour. How often does such a thing happen I wonder?

4. 'I haven't had much luck with men,' Rebecca said as we waved her and Tony off to a new life. 'But I think this time will be different,' she said, smiling in Tony's direction. And different it proved to be. Not long after settling into their new town – jobs secured, tentative friendships forming – the police knocked on the door, one warm evening. Took Tony away for a crime committed long ago, well before Rebecca had met him. It was a serious crime. He would not be coming back any time soon. 'I haven't had much luck with men,' Rebecca said.

5. 'This is the worst decision I have ever made!' That's Margot, protagonist in *Cat Person*, a short story by Kristen Roupenian, published in December 2017. Whether fiction or nonfiction, good pieces of writing can make a connection to our own experiences. We might see ourselves in the scene, or perhaps feel it as the characters have felt it. Perhaps it just gets us thinking. Which is what happened when I read *Cat Person*. The 'worst decision' is the thought that enters Margot's mind immediately after Robert has finished having sex with her.

Margot is a 20-year old student working part-time in a cinema where she meets Robert, an older customer. The two start a friendship of sorts with a lot of texting in a getting-to-know-each-other sort of way before going on a date: movie, drinks and back to Robert's place.

Late in the scene Margot reappraises the situation. She doesn't find Robert, or the thought of what is to come appealing, but not having the capacity to put a stop to it, she sees it through to the end, and that 'worst decision' moment.

The piece is written in the third person. To Margot: 'The thought of stopping what she had set in motion was overwhelming. It would require an amount of tact and gentleness that she felt was impossible to summon.'

How often, I wondered, does that happen. How often might women, probably more so than men, tell themselves they agreed to sex to avoid accepting they had no choice. How broad is the grey area of sexual consent?

The story went viral and attracted those who saw it from Margot's point of view and those who saw it from Robert's point of view. There is a power imbalance between the two, but it goes both ways. Margot is young, attractive and educated with an interest in the world. She might see Robert as cute, or interesting, but he doesn't have the same outlook and is a little disdainful of her college-girl status. Margot is able to put the episode behind her. Robert is not. He sulkily accepts she doesn't want to continue the relationship before becoming abusive via text message.

Verbal abuse is often a precursor to physical abuse.

I write from the perspective, the security, of a long and happy relationship. But you never stop learning and reading *Cat Person* got me thinking of my own experience. Have I ever had sex with someone who might have thought they had no way out of it, no way of saying: 'Sorry, I've changed my mind?' Someone who felt a power imbalance, or went through with it to avoid hurting my feelings, just as Margot could not find the tact or gentleness needed to get out of her situation?

The honest answer is I don't know, though it must be possible. I suspect I'm not the only one to have these thoughts, but if I am, I shouldn't be.

6. While camping in Mutawintji National Park, on a trip through western New South Wales in 2015, I climbed the Bynguano Range late

one afternoon for the sunset. I had been thinking about the degraded landscape, largely cleared of timber years earlier for the Broken Hill smelters, and was intending to make some notes with the idea of writing on that. Instead, I found myself thinking on the lives some people lead. This forced itself into a poem.

CHILD DEVELOPMENT: IN FOUR PARTS

1. DAY OUT

>You'd promised a day out,
>a good day out.
>>Away from the noise, the motion,
>>the temptation and usual habits.
>
>>>Out of town,
>>>down on the river.
>
>Started well with a swim,
>then watched the kids play,
>>while you got close to their mum.
>>That'd been a while.
>
>Things turned at lunch,
>when you drank too much.
>>Lost your cool with the kids,
>>and then with their mum.
>
>Who had to drive home,
>which was … okay.
>>Until your car ran out of petrol.
>>Out of mobile range.

>   'That can't be,' you protested,
>   'I put twenty dollars in just the other day.'
>
> Then, as the kids fell quiet in the back seat,
> and while the motor ticked, you heard a muttering:
>   'I'm fucking over this,
>   I'm fucking over you.'
>
> Now, while your gut churned,
> with that familiar sinking feeling,
>   you hung your head low,
>   knowing you'd done it again.

2. MELANIE

> She had sworn off men, more than once.
> Now, with calculated intent,
> kids at school, curtains drawn,
> she took him into her bed for the first time.
>
> In his lost eyes she had seen herself.
> A yearning affinity, the promise of kinship.
> Though by the time she realised she didn't know him at all,
> it was too late.
>
> Buried also, among the habits of time, life's fractures
> and wrong turns, it was plain.
> The person she knew least, was herself. She was alien
> to herself. As a child.

3. DARREN

'Some trauma,' they say, 'is so deep it possesses but can never be possessed.'
Acting as if it doesn't exist is an act of psychological denial, cloaked in self-preservation.
Perfectly rational.

Some acts are so shameful, others, even those close, can only turn away.
'Time and space heal,' they say.
They are wrong.

Try though, he will. Moving restlessly, as a tumbleweed, from town to town.
Seeking solace in drink, drugs, fleeting friendships.
Failed relationships.

And always the refrain: 'It wasn't my fault.'
Destined to remain a child.

4. JAY (13 YEARS) AND AMBER (8 YEARS)

'Here we go again,'
Jay thinks, squeezing Amber's hand,
staring straight ahead,
'another melt down,'
knowing that once again,
he will have to put the pieces back together,
he will have to be the adult.

Consequences

Life writing can be hard.

The opening to this part of the book was a brief and stark account of the beginning of my marriage. Throughout that short marriage there were plenty of highlights, or downlights, to choose from but just a few key events have been selected here.

Memoir is an account of how the writer experienced their life and its events, with honesty at its heart. What I have written is honest in its recollection and its reflections on what it all meant. It is written without bitterness, I have none, but I don't deny the sadness. That's how it is.

Not everyone experiences events the same way. Acknowledging that others may have experienced it differently shows self-awareness and is a fair and right thing to do. It may build confidence or trust in the unfolding story.

I once saw a review of a published memoir where the critic thought the memoirist held back, was too restrained. I remember the part that said if your first instinct is to button your lip, why would you bother?

I said earlier that memoir is almost exclusively written in first person, but in writing about traumatic or painful events it can help to take ourselves out of the frame, to write from the point of view of an outside observer. This may be someone who was there, such as a neighbour, a friend or a police officer. Or it might be an imaginary observer. They may take an objective point of view, recounting the facts, or a subjective point of view where their opinion is clear. They may take an all-knowing omniscient point of view where their wisdom is clear in explaining events. That writing would be in third person: 'he, she' or 'they' felt something; rather than first person, 'I' felt something. With some time and distance for reconciling with the events, a way may become clear to re-write it in the first person. Or it may not. Some of what I have written in the personal essay that follows is in third person. Sometimes it's just easier that way.

IN LIFE THERE IS LUCK

On New Year's Day 2004 I was headed east along the Eyre Highway, after a couple of months work and holiday in West Australia. Most people, I suspect, see the Nullarbor Plain as an endurance test. Something to be traversed as quickly as possible. And for many, living there might be something of an endurance test as well. As I entered a Nullarbor Plains roadhouse a woman shouted through the back door, 'Hey love, there's a fellow on the phone. Wants to know if a woman with two kids in a Subaru has been through.'

These words are imprinted on my brain, for more than 20 years before that Nullarbor Plains fuel stop, I had been the fellow on the phone.

This is a story of a short marriage – a marriage of little contentment but plenty of resentment – and its aftermath. Its beginning is essentially a story of kids having kids. While there was love it was not a mature love. It had no capacity to evolve, as people and relationships inevitably do. When things went bad, which didn't take long, there was no capacity for a resolution. No role model, no life skills to draw on.

Late night, a bit pissed, he returned home. The broken home. Here, she too a bit pissed, was waiting to go out. 'The kids are in bed,' she said, 'I'll be back in the morning,' grabbing her keys. An argument ensued. No rhyme nor reason to this argument. No exchange of new information, no new insights gleaned. Just a rehash. After a while she decided she wasn't going out after all. No rhyme nor reason to that either, just doing what he now didn't want.

He pushed. She fell. You bastard, she said. Quickly back on her feet, and with another change of mind out to the car.

Next morning she returned. Few words were exchanged. He went to work, feeling fully churned as he had done for weeks. Pushing her, as he had done, went against his core. He didn't *do that*, though he had. He would apologise when he got home. It wouldn't fix things, this marriage was beyond fixable, but saying sorry was the right thing to do. And something had to give. They couldn't stay in the same house and had to work that out.

Some say intuition is a sixth sense. As soon as he pulled up that afternoon, he sensed something wasn't right. Entering the house he went straight to the kid's bedroom. A few scattered toys on the floor, the favourite blankets missing. In the bedroom they had once shared the wardrobe and dresser were emptied of most of her clothes.

Gone.

'She's not here. I don't know where she is. No, I haven't seen her. Yes, I'll tell her you called if I see her.' Friends' words he didn't believe.

Later that night he drove around town. Parked away from street lights and peered into backyards, looking for her car. Nowhere.

Next morning he started. Katherine, Larrimah, Elliott, Tenant Creek, calling all the roadhouses, 'Has a woman with two kids in a Toyota been through?'

The guilt lingered. Because of his actions she had fled. This had not been heavy-duty violence, but it was an act of violence and it weighed heavily.

Many months later, going through the legal motions, a solicitor noted her social security claim. It had been lodged some weeks before the push. And at that time, she had given her parents' address, in another state.

The move had been well planned in advance. This offered some balm to his conscience, but the balm was thinly applied. Perhaps she had planned to tell him of her plans to leave, and his actions had just bought the departure forward. Unlikely, he thought, but possible.

No way of knowing, but offering this small benefit of the doubt had the advantage of holding onto the guilt, now a constant companion. Self-punishment becomes a virtue.

As marriage collapses go, mine may have been nothing out of the ordinary, but I experienced it badly. The empty house was too much. I had trouble being there. For a while I regularly slept in the car, or at the beach. And then, with too much time alone the dog rebelled. He too, abandoned me. Everyone's left, I now thought.

Most of my friendships I came to see as shallow. Those that may have been genuine I may have rejected. I started to find being alone suited me. Prone to bouts of depression and drinking to excess, I didn't cope.

Sometime later when respite had come, though temporarily it turned out, I made a conscious decision not to try and see the kids until they had grown up – more than a dozen years away. Then, I'd find them and explain how it had been for me and why I had made the decision. While thinking it through, I knew with absolute certainty I would come to regret this decision. But I made it anyway. I had a certain talent for knowingly making bad decisions.

I have one clear memory of the day, the very first day, when I realised that the previous day I had given no thought to my kids. The feeling of that day, and its conflicting emotions of relief and shame, is strong. But beyond knowing it was in Darwin, and therefore within just a few years of their leaving, I can't say when or where.

> Not a moment's thought had been given
> the day before, to the loss that had followed
> like a heavy shadow.

And so, what comes next?
Relief you may think, but no,
despair instead.
And it proves enduring, gaining weight
over the years, as it's clutched tight,
bringing a strange balm.
Replacing the loss with
a smothering, but curiously comforting,
blanket of shame.

A few years on, after some periods of illusory inner peace, I reacted to the latest turmoil, and what may have been a little bit of a break down, in the only way I knew how. Bailed out on an impulse and caught a bus to Cairns.

Another couple of years on I wrote a letter. The enormity of my bad decision-making had long sunk in. I made it clear I didn't want to cause any distress, but if it were possible, I'd like to make contact with the kids.

I'm eternally grateful their mother said yes. She didn't have to do that. Soon enough I went up from Sydney, where I was then living, to the NSW north coast for a weekend visit. The eldest had a vague memory of me, or at least of someone else in his life. The youngest had no such memory. They called someone else dad, but the time together that weekend was as good as I could have hoped for. They were understandably reluctant but we grew just a little closer over that weekend. When we parted, after goodbyes in a garage carpark, I cried like I'd never cried before.

Over the next years I saw them regularly for a while, then sporadically. I was conscious of not trying to be the back-again-father, didn't see that I had any natural rights. I had few parenting skills and couldn't manage to form a friendship. There was little capacity to strengthen tenuous bonds. In a nutshell, they didn't have a great time when with me, which came to a head one visit.

The choice between a few days in a tent with me, or the caravan with their mother and her husband, along with the full range of creature comforts and other kids to play with, was a no-brainer. I went back to my camp alone. Drank myself to a steady oblivion and slept on the beach, unable to face the empty tent and the kids toys I had waiting there.

As they matured, and they have long been grown men, they have made their rational decisions which I have come to accept. This acceptance has not been reached easily. It's caused much grief, more than I'm going to recount here. Too many years apart, too little in common and too many other more suitable male role models in their lives. That's the reality. I am unimportant to them.

On point of view

People have sometimes said they feel self-conscious writing their life story with 'I,' which may be a form of reverse narcissism. While starting each paragraph with 'I,' or having this liberally sprinkled throughout the writing would be tedious, it's what I, you and other readers of memoir expect.

The second person point of view is 'you' or 'they,' which provides distance and is a little murkier, not as vivid.

Third person point of view is 'she' or 'they,' or It might be 'the girl,' or 'Rebecca,' who went out for the evening or whatever it was they did, which can seem uncomfortable, perhaps a little aloof. Or outright self-centred, such as when people refer to themselves in the third person. Pompous perhaps.

Writing in the third person offers the opportunity to present an objective, dispassionate portrayal of people and events. Telling it as it is, or was. A journalistic style reporting offers some breathing space, not exactly de-personalising it, but easing the tension. The third person also allows an omniscient, all knowing all seeing, authoritative point of view. This may well suit a story of personal development from childhood to adulthood, a story of particular behaviours, or anywhere an explanatory voice is needed.

Discovery

The nature or nurture dichotomy I opened this chapter with could be usefully applied to the northern parts of Australia, where many people's default response towards those 'down south' is to heap scorn, if not loathe and detest them.

An argument may be possible that this is nature for those born or long resident in the north, but many of those newly resident in the north are readily nurtured. Perhaps that may be part of fitting in. 'We vote for the Nat's up here,' conservative retirees from Victoria have long been told on arrival to the Queensland coast. There's probably a PhD in that for someone.

I have lived in both the north and the south, so I wasn't surprised at the response from my new work colleagues in Brisbane and elsewhere in Queensland to a proposal from Canberra that opens this personal essay.

In January 1990 I started work as education officer at Greening Australia, a national environmental organisation with a focus on land and vegetation management and restoration. I was based in Brisbane when my counterpart in Canberra called with an invitation to be part of a national education project. Greening Australia works as a federation and all states and territories were invited to contribute to the project. I ran it past a few people and got back to my counterpart, politely declining: 'No thanks, the feeling is it won't work in Queensland.' The response was terse, to say the least.

A Greening Australia education officer's network was established with meetings two or three times a year, which provided the chance to look at what worked and what didn't and develop a national perspective.

One of these meetings, in September 1992, was arranged to coincide with an environmental education conference in Perth. A few of us took some extra days, traipsing around the wild flowers and wine areas south of Perth before the conference. I headed north for a few days after the conference with a colleague. Spring flowering in West Australia is all they say it is, and travel to both the south and the north of Perth, as we did, is to discover two entirely different and changing landscapes. Not the only discovery, as it turned out.

⁓

Although living some distance apart we saw each other a few times a year and spoke regularly. At meetings and conferences we started to seek out each other's company. We talked about our work, it's similarities and differences. Our successes and failures. About the joys and wonders of our education officers' network of eight, four with an education background and four with horticultural backgrounds. About managing the expectations of others with different needs: conservative farmers, environmentalists, teachers, government agency workers.

We discovered shared world views, liked a drink together, the occasional cigar. Preferred something more exotic than the meat and three veg we had grown up on. We also liked a challenge, taking pleasure in the unexpected and the absurd, with a preference to make it up as you go along. We could spot pretentious bullshit and bureaucratic nonsense. We became close. All entirely platonic.

On our travels south and then north of Perth little thought was given to the sharing of motel rooms, with two single beds. On our first day out heading south, suffering a lack of sleep and perhaps a slight hangover, she had slept, while I drove.

Talk comes easy in the bubble of a car. A rapport can be established, or in our case strengthened. Intimacies are easily shared, vulnerabilities exposed, hopes laid out. And we did a lot of driving that weekend heading north after the Perth conference. Off firstly to Cervantes, a small fishing village near the ancient rock pillars and sand dunes of The Pinnacles National Park. After that Kalbarri, Geraldton, Dongara and then back to Perth.

We discovered similar family upbringings. Insecurities and vulnerabilities were laid out, tentatively at first. Then more elaborately, more fully. Suggestions made. Affirmations: 'Yes, that's happened to me,' or 'I don't think I could have done any better.'

Life's fuck-ups were explored. She agreed with me on my big mistake, without judging, just accepting. I had rarely told anyone of this. A mutual admiration society was forming.

I left Perth on the red-eye back to Sydney, and then up to Brisbane, with a head cold that went to my sinus bringing on a thumping headache, and a mixed bag of emotions. Delight at the connection, the acceptance, but turmoil at the uncertainty. One party to an evolving relationship being married with three kids can do that.

We knew we had options. We could continue to meet a few times a year, perhaps carry on an affair. But that would be unsatisfying and almost certainly end in tears. Neither of us needed that. A few days later we spoke. 'There's a lot of reasons why we shouldn't be together,' I said, 'but geography isn't one of them.'

A new start for both of us was laid out. She would leave her long-standing marriage, long-standing but failed – which her husband would acknowledge – but this would be done in an orderly fashion. There would be no hysterics, a minimum of drama. I recall being amazed at this woman's honesty. I had expected to be brought into her kid's thinking at some stage, probably not too far distant, just not now. But they were told of me and my place in their changing word, gently but plainly I have no doubt, from the start.

On any of my work trips I would find time, usually plenty of time, to do my own thing. Between one town and the next I regularly took the back road or detoured for a walk in a nature reserve or park. Sometimes I pulled over at a historical marker, or an interesting tree or creek. Occasionally I played music, loud. Nothing like the Drummers of Burundi when you have the place to yourself. Or a cup of tea while I sat quietly, watching, listening, contemplating. And then, suddenly, I had a letter to write.

The letter was often a reflection, an update on the latest conversation, and these were frequent now. Putting thoughts into words, putting it down on paper, made it permanent, something for the archive, as it turned out. Writing is thinking, refined thinking, and I, we, had plenty of thinking to do. This was reinforcement: planning, explaining, asking, understanding, deepening, wondering, creating. This was being open: no place, no need, for secrets.

A couple of months after the discovery of that trip to WA – on Boxing Day 1993 – I met Meg at Brisbane airport. I like to say we personalised a professional relationship. And my colleague from Canberra was no longer terse with me.

One day I'll return to the archive.

For several years I had been self-reflective, perhaps obsessively so. I was largely disinterested in any sort of relationship, except on occasion the briefest kind. I suspect I may have carried an aura of damage and probably didn't have too much to worry about. There was no queue and I was quite unsettled, moving somewhere new every few years. Never going back. But I knew I didn't want a relationship that went through the motions. It had to be something special, or not at all. And now I had something I knew was special. I had learnt a few things in all that solitude but there's always more to learn.

After some time around Brisbane, and a little further north turtle watching at Mon Repos near Bundaberg, we were headed south to Canberra, taking our time. Talking, or enjoying the companionable silence. There was a particular point as we headed down the range steeply from Dorrigo to Bellingen, through rainforest and lush farming land, when something was said. I don't recall what it was or even who said it, but it was pointed, maybe a little barbed. We had spent more than a week together and perhaps we were finding more about each other's soft spots. Perhaps we were just learning how to be together.

'That hit a nerve,' Meg said, or something similar. And it had. An uncomfortable and pivotal moment crystallised before me. I recognised I could take the easy path. If I'm being honest, and I may as well be, this would involve taking offence, perhaps a sullen withdrawal. I well knew what the inside of my shell looked like.

Or I could let it go, which I chose to do, and felt something close to euphoria. If we had been in bed, I would have touched her foot with mine, to show I'd let it go, that it would be all right. Instead I rested my hand on her thigh. She was driving after all.

Meg's kids, 13, 11 and nine at the time, were confused and not a little upset. They were provided the full story from the start and acknowledged that Meg had been unhappy, often angry in the marriage. Given the choice they opted to stay with their father, visiting and staying with Meg (and me) regularly. Meg accepted this as their choice. There was no pressure from her and she trusted them to work it out. They did so, quite quickly, and have a strong relationship with their mother. At varying rates they came to accept me. I have long known their love, which I return, with gratitude.

Many, if not most, of the friends from the marriage directed their allegiance to the abandoned husband. Few managed to retain friendship with both, although some have since returned. This was hurtful, but accepted with grace. What was perhaps harder, was the attitude of Meg's parents, whose loyalty went to the husband.

Through all of this Meg never wavered. When people said how sorry they were to hear the marriage had ended she told them not to be. She was happy now, which she hadn't been for a long time.

And me? I'm a better person for having observed and for being part of this. I can't help but admire and learn from the integrity and the composure

Meg brought to this most difficult of situations. A situation where she had so much to lose if things didn't work out. And only me to gain.

I said earlier that life writing can be hard. It can also be joyous and re-affirming, which I found here. And it can be nerve-wracking. I was surprised at how nervous I was, waiting outside a motel room in central Victoria, while Meg read this passage. She knew she had full right of veto, but used none of it. 'Beautiful,' she said.

Family history

'Look at this,' Meg said while fossicking through the oddments at a garage sale one weekend in 2015. 'It's an old postcard of Sicily.' We were planning a trip to Europe and Sicily was in our thinking. But Meg didn't have her glasses on. It was actually an old concertina-style postcard of the Scilly Isles.

I had long been vaguely aware of a family connection with the Scilly Isles. When my parents built a new house in 1970 an old ship's bell appeared by the front door. It was a great grandfather (or someone down the rabbit hole of Gibson family history) who had been a ship's captain in the Scilly Isles before coming to Australia I was told, with no further detail offered, no story laid out. I enquired no further. The disinterest of youth.

We flipped through the black and white concertina photos of a town, beaches, a flower farm, a castle, and then, there on the back:

JAMES GIBSON,
SCILLY ISLES.
Copyright.

A couple of years after discovering the postcard we are on a boat leaving Penzance on the south-west tip of England for the three hour crossing to the Scilly Isles. These are an archipelago of 140 odd islands and islets situated at the western end of the British Channel. Here, the strong influence of the North Atlantic Current, or Gulf Stream, makes for a much milder current than the mainland: warmer in winter, cooler in summer. It's a grey, cool and windy day with limited visibility until we approach the Isles, mostly low, rocky and covered in heath, with many sandy beaches.

After booking in for a couple of nights at the Atlantic Hotel in Hugh Town, on the main island of St Mary's, we wander around getting our bearings. Coffee is followed by a picnic lunch in a local park. We then come across a local art and craft fair and are quite taken by a painting of an island beach scene, just like what we had seen from the boat. Chatting to a lady as we purchased it, I mentioned my family connection. 'You should go and see Roger,' she said, 'He'll know something. You can find him through the museum.'

The Isles of Scilly Museum has an extensive collection from pre-history to the present including ship-wrecks, archaeological sites and family history records. It also has excellent volunteers, one of whom directs us across the road to Roger and Kathy Banfield's home.

Busy people are Roger and Kathy, and I have to call several times before finding them at home. They are immediately interested and willing to help, sharing a few snippets of Gibson family history, before arranging to meet at the museum the day after next.

When we meet as pre-arranged Roger leads us to the nearby old Wesleyan Church. 'Something you should see before we start,' he says, leading us upstairs to a stained glass window with a dedication: 'Presented by children and grandchildren of Stephen and Elizabeth Gibson, of South Australia, for 59 years service.'

I come from a small family where there had been little contact with extended family. While growing up there were no family stories of the achievements, adventures or mischiefs of various descendants. I had little interest until, as happens, I grew older. And now, I am wondering.

James Gibson, he of our postcard, was third in a family line of four photographers from the Scilly Isles, the family being distantly related to my birth family. The first of the photographers, John, lived from 1827 to 1920. Shortly after his father had died, when John was 12, he went to sea to contribute to the family finances. On one of his trips abroad John bought his first camera, quite a luxury in those times. And that's how it started. By his mid-thirties John had established a photographic studio in Penzance. Within a few years he returned to St. Mary's establishing another photographic studio.

John, and the following three generations of photographers, systematically recorded more than 200 shipwrecks and rescue attempts in the waters of the Scilly Isles and west Cornwall. These are some of the most treacherous waters in the Atlantic. The first of the shipwrecks was in 1869, the same year the telegraph arrived in the Scilly Isles. Acting as a local news correspondent, John was able to send written details on the identity of the ship, the number of survivors and the rescue attempt, becoming a pioneer of photojournalism. To get to the shipwrecks usually required significant effort of cross country or open boat travel, taking along cumbersome equipment: a heavy camera, chemicals, glass plates and a portable darkroom. And all this in shipwreck weather.

John employed his sons, Alexander, born in 1857, and Herbert, born 1861, as apprentices. The two brothers had wildly different temperaments, with Alexander noted as being creative, flamboyant even, while Herbert was more reserved and became the backbone of the business. After Alexander's death in 1944, his son James took over the business, which coincided with the transition to film. Apart from shipwrecks, the business recorded daily life and significant community or personal events throughout the Scilly's. Some of these photographs made their way into souvenirs such as calendars and postcards, including the one we discovered 30 odd years after James' death in 1985.

James' son Frank carried on the business until he died in 2012. In 2013 England's National Maritime Museum purchased the Gibson photographic archive at auction. This is a social history collection of over

1,300 glass plate and film negatives, showing not just the scene of the shipwreck but the human impact. The responses of shipwreck survivors and local people to rescue and salvage efforts, successes and failures, are well captured. Although the family no longer has a photographic business, Frank's daughter, Sandra Kyne, runs a gift shop in St Mary's, using many of the family's images in calendars, postcards and souvenirs.

So, who is this Stephen Gibson from the church window? And what's his connection to the ship's bell at our Eden Hills front door? And what is the original Gibson connection to the Scilly Isles? Roger has many of these answers.

Turns out a John Gibson, who was born in Scotland around 1700, had probably arrived in the Scilly Isles by 1724. The family story is that he was on his way to America, at that time rife with opportunities for making a fortune, but became seasick and asked to be put ashore in Scilly Isles. The main island, St Marys, had a busy port with lots of trade opportunities, but he settled on St Martins, one of the outer islands with very little settlement, and little to offer apart from fishing, potatoes and kelp-burning.

So why would someone intending to travel to America, presumably in search of a fortune, settle in such an isolated place with limited opportunities? Theories are that he may have been a deserter from the army or navy, or may have been fleeing disorder in Scotland where Jacobite Rebels had been at civil war with the government. Whatever the real reason, St Martins would have suited someone who didn't want to be noticed.

Sometime before 1726 John married Joan, whose surname is unknown, but who probably came from St Martins or nearby Tresco. They had nine or ten children. At the time of his death in St Martins in 1765 John left a large sum of money, more than 100 pounds, to his wife, and upon her death, to the surviving children and grandchildren. On Joan's death, about 1793, the money is missing. This causes friction between John and Joan's children, leading to court action.

Another question though, is how did John amass such a large amount of money? Kelp-burning, fishing and growing potatoes seems unlikely, with a large family to support. Did he bring the money with him from Scotland? Smuggling was a lucrative business in those days, and later descendants were involved in this. But can someone badly affected by seasickness be a smuggler? Or perhaps his smuggling activities were land based. But from an outer island of the Scilly Isles? Ship-wreck bounty is another possibility. But this is all conjecture.

Several generations on we come to Stephen Gibson, born in 1800. In 1824 he married Elizabeth May who had been born in 1799. That's Stephen and Elizabeth of the church window. They had three children, Stephen junior born in 1825, Elizabeth born in 1827 and Catherine born in 1836.

Some time after she married, daughter Elizabeth and her husband migrated to South Australia, while Stephen junior and Catherine stayed on the Scilly Isles with their parents. Catherine married a master mariner, Thomas Cook Hicks, who along with a couple of other members of the Gibson and Cook Hicks families was lost at sea off Cape Horn in 1874. Soon after this family tragedy, Elizabeth's husband died in South Australia.

In 1880, still with a great deal of grief between them, Stephen and Elizabeth, now in their 80s, along with Stephen junior and his second wife, Jane Cook Hicks, and the now widowed Catherine, all migrated to South Australia. A number of other members of the Cook Hicks family travelled with them.

Along with a smuggler or two, many men of the Gibson family have been seamen, several losing their lives at sea, a couple receiving gold watches from different United States presidents for their valour in aiding in the rescue of American boats, shipwrecked or in peril. Stephen senior was the first Captain of the *Lady of the Isles*, a ship plying between the Scilly Isles and Penzance. Stephen junior was also a mariner. The appearance of the ship's bell by the front door of the Eden Hills house becomes more explicable.

The Gibson family of photographers, who sparked this inquiry are only distantly related. The common ancestry goes back to John, who came from Scotland.

I've heard what family history can do to people, so how do I feel about my family heritage? More curious than excited I have to say, though it is quite a fascinating story, which in another family may have been told around the kitchen table.

As we are leaving the museum, with a bundle of information, Roger tells us much of this had been collected by a Gibson family descendant from Australia who had visited ten years earlier and spent a month in the Scilly Isles carrying out research. Roger gives us an email address for Gina Francis, who, it turns out, lives about 40 kilometres from where I live. I'll be in touch, I say. I am not looking to establish a family or make connections where there have been none, but I am curious.

The phone call

After the first eight years of our relationship in Canberra, Meg and I moved to the New South Wales south coast in 2001. Huskisson is a village of about 900 people on Jervis Bay, 200 kilometres or so south of Sydney. The stunning natural environment was the main appeal, nicely balanced by a slightly daggy townscape. More shabby than shabby chic. And while we liked living there, we never thought of it as the forever place. It wasn't, as many locals liked to call it, paradise.

That stunning natural environment though, like so many other places, is blighted by a rapacious development mentality buttressed by the divide and conquer approach of the local council.

> White sand, blue water, bush all around. Nature at its best, how sublime.
>
> Ha! What this place needs is more development. Now's the time.

From the beginning of our time together Meg and I consciously aimed for a fun committed relationship. The serious part would demand and receive attention in its own good time, but it didn't deserve a focus. The relationship was built on the twin foundations of support and independence. A sort of inter-dependence, if you like, along with the desire for personal growth, new experiences. We had our own acronym for each other: B F & L, or Best Friend and Lover.

In June 2015, while Meg was staying in a converted butter factory 250 kilometres down the coast with friends for a few days, and I was in the *jardin habitacion* – the name we gave to the renovated shed in the back yard – one of our phone conversations went something like this;

> It's lovely down here. But bloody cold where we are staying.
>
> Yes, I'd like to have a closer look around there some time.
>
> Maybe we should come down together some time soon.
>
> Let's do it.

The conversation moved on to whatever it moved on to, quite likely something about the latest development proposal and the council bending over backwards to support it, before the next day's conversation included something like this;

> I had a look in some real estate windows today. Pretty interesting around here …
>
> Yes. I had a look on-line …

And that was pretty much it. Without either of us raising the possibility of moving on from Huskisson, we had each come to the same thought at the same time.

At Huskisson we lived about 400 metres from the beach, a beautiful beach. We liked that beach, swam there most of the year, and swam, not just splashed about. But we didn't need to be so close to the beach any more.

A couple of scouting trips down the coast proved fruitless. We didn't find anything we liked. And then the penny dropped. Why, we wondered, were we aiming to move from one environment to another very similar environment? Where's the adventure in that? What about the other direction? For family reasons New South Wales was our scope. We quickly ruled out any of the larger coastal towns and the Hunter Valley with its lunar landscape was a no-no for us.

Somehow Kyogle came up. A small town in northern New South Wales 40 kilometres north-west of the larger city of Lismore. We had passed through Kyogle several times previously, stopped for coffee or lunch and visited some of the nearby national parks. But hadn't spent any real time there. So exactly why it came to mind is a mystery.

We had a six-week trip through western NSW and south-east Queensland coming up and decided to have a close look at Kyogle on the way back. And then we discovered it was just as we recalled. A main road from south to north with a sumptuous rising bend at either end of town. A stretch of art deco buildings lining the central area. Few franchise businesses and nothing pretentious. A general air of satisfaction with itself and public toilets that stay open overnight.

And Kyogle is where we moved to in January 2016. Out of harm's way we call it. A bit of a backwater, on a main road to nowhere much. Away from the constant madness of coastal development. Here, in Kyogle, watching property prices is not an obsession as it was, is, for many on the coast. Don't get me wrong, we did well out of real estate. Sold on the coast for, relatively speaking, a lot, and bought inland, for, relatively speaking, not much. But property values are not our focus.

As I write this, five years on from that phone conversation, I feel very self-satisfied at how we reached that decision – time to move on – independently but simultaneously. Says something about the relationship. I could almost be smug, but I know what preceded it, and I know not everyone is that fortunate.

I've had a crook back

... just like the 16 per cent of Australians who have back problems at any one time, and the more than 70 per cent who will suffer lower back pain at some stage of their life.

My crook back, at its crookest, lasted more than a year. It had its ups and downs and caused a lot of grief. And not just to me. Lack of sleep and the pain may have contributed to a lost sense of humour. Or so I've been told. And don't deny. Intense pain saw me at the emergency department at four o'clock one morning, having been awake all night.

I have tried most everything: physiotherapy, acupuncture, shiatsu therapy, chiropractic treatment, ortho-bionomy, osteopathy, Bowen therapy. Along with these, a once only visit to a naturopath and his electromagnetic machine which was almost certain to fix me he claimed; and failing this stem cell treatment in Beijing was guaranteed to work.

I've done prescription medicines, herbal medicine, Chinese medicine, cortisone injections, arnica and comfrey cream, tiger balm and cannabis tincture (purchased at a pre-arranged meeting by the recycling station opposite the shopping centre). Hot packs, ice packs, a Transcutaneous Electrical Nerve Stimulation Device. A mindfulness course.

X-rays and MRI scan reports bring a new mystifying terminology that can sound positively scary. Anterolisthesis is a slipped vertebra. Spondylitis is inflammation of one or more vertebrae. Hemangioma is a benign tumour. Stenosis is a narrowing of the spaces within the spine, putting pressure on the nerves that travel through the spine. Tell me about it.

The Health Service Pain Clinic was four hours a week for six weeks with a psychologist, a physiotherapist and a bunch of other people with chronic pain. I started that program thinking I was way better off than the others, even wondering if I should be there. I finished that program thinking I was way worse off than the others. No reflection on the Pain Clinic, just the ups and downs of my crook back.

The Pain Clinic approach includes building knowledge and understanding of back pain, de-sensitisation and breathing techniques. Chronic pain lasts beyond normal injury healing time, usually more than three months. Acute pain is of shorter duration but gradually resolves as the injury heals.

Like all new terminology this can be difficult as one person, in great distress, at the first of the Pain Clinic sessions let known: 'Don't tell me this is chronic pain,' he said, 'this is really fucking acute.'

I've been told I have the trifecta of back problems. Broad based bulging discs. Most people settle for one. A slipped vertebra. Narrowing of the spinal column which puts pressure on the nerve. And it's nerve pain I have had, down the leg into the foot. Curiously little pain in my back. It's all referred. These conditions are topped-up by osteoarthritis and other minor bits and pieces of degeneration. After obscuring my name one of my practitioners took my MRI scans to his students at university. I'm a case study.

You must have had a major trauma to get that much damage, I heard. No, I've never had a major car accident. Never fallen out of a tree and landed on my tailbone. Just cumulative, slow damage over several decades. Young and invincible I used to be. And bloody silly I know now. There's a lot of advantages to getting older, it's said. But none of them are physical.

I've done the gamut of anti-inflammatories and pain killers. Panadeine Forte had no effect. Lyrica, prescribed mainly for nerve pain, seemed a good thing. Started at 25mg to no effect. Upped to 75mg and then 300mg. Still nothing. Antenex to relieve muscle spasms, the anti-inflammatory Panafcortelone, Moxicam for osteoarthritis and Nupentin for neuropathic pain. Nothing made a dent until the early morning trip to emergency. Here I was given a new painkiller, Endone.

Go home, the nurse said, and if you are still in pain in half an hour come back (the joys of a small town). Otherwise come back at eight and see the doctor. I went home and slept the most beautiful of sleeps. At eight I went back and left with a script for Endone, my very best new friend. Take one, four times a day as needed.

Endone is the brand name for Oxycodone hydrochloride, a narcotic, like morphine, heroin and codeine. It was originally used for late stage cancer pain before becoming more widely prescribed. There has been much recent inquiry into the use of this medicine with a general consensus it's over-prescribed. While it can and does work for acute or short-term pain, it doesn't work in the longer term for chronic or on-going pain.

Its effectiveness wears off quite quickly. People take more to try and compensate for falling effectiveness. They may become addicted. They may overdose. Many do. In 2017 during my experience with Endone, I learnt that around 1,400 people die from overdosing on prescription opioids each month in the United States, where it was described as a national emergency.

I used it as recommended, taking one up to four times a day, for several days and then started to cut back. After a few weeks I was down to just one, before bed, which let me sleep. A couple of weeks on I decided to try and sleep without it, but woke after a few hours. My friend, Endone, out in the kitchen, was calling me: 'Come out, we're here for you. You know we'll help you sleep. You want to sleep, don't you?' Endone didn't want to end our friendship. This monologue went on for some time, but somehow or other I prevailed. The pain clinic's psychologist had heard of this. He likened it to hallucinating.

I need information. I've read extensively, trawling the internet. I've asked questions and strived to understand the answers. 'Think out loud,' has been my request of my various practitioners as they have plied their trade. Several of these have said they see a lot of people who don't want to do anything between treatments, they don't want to know anything. They just want to be fixed. A level of outsourcing I don't get.

I've seen neuro-surgeons, not because I wanted surgery, but because I need to know my options. There are two common forms of spinal surgery. A lumbar laminectomy, sometimes called decompression, removes bone and tissue to open the spinal canal and remove pressure on the nerves. Both neuro-surgeons were happy to perform this procedure in the private health system. One of them also works in a public hospital. I was told he would not be permitted to operate on me in the public system as my case was not severe enough and there were other therapies to be pursued. Money buys most things.

The other far more extensive surgery is spinal fusion, which permanently joins two or more vertebrae to stabilise the spine. In 2017/18 almost 18,000 spinal fusion surgeries were carried out in Australia.

There is growing evidence that this is not the best option for many people suffering back pain. It doesn't always work and can leave people worse off. As with many things in a free market economy the medical system incentivises surgery, which leads to a potential conflict of interest.

There has been little support for non-operative procedures but there is growing evidence that structured physical therapy programs and cognitive behaviour therapy are as good as spinal fusion. We are talking on-going management, not a cure for the problem. There is no fix.

I've shed tears over this crook back of mine. Tears of pain, tears of frustration. Of helplessness. I sat on the steps of one of my practitioners who had just delivered the news he couldn't help me anymore, and, feeling like I'd been sacked, I wept. Deeply. I had never known pain could stop the ability to think clearly. This was just constant awful pain, only broken by occasional surges. Even at my lowest point I was never suicidal, but I have come to understand how some people could be. I can't imagine going through that whole experience without love and support and enough money to pay for the various treatments I tried. Keep on trying, don't give up, don't be a victim was the approach taken.

And now, I'm winning. I can't say I've won and I'm never going to have a great back. It needs ongoing attention but it's going to serve me well enough. I made it back to the tennis court and, happily, my sense of humour has returned. Persistence could be one of my defining traits.

Financial literacy

While growing up in 1960s suburban Adelaide my parents provided weekly pocket money, which helped as I entered the economy. I don't recall having to do much around the house to earn a pay. Having cash was a status symbol and I needed status to deal with the growing pains of the teenage years. When the parental offering wasn't enough I nicked some more. Only small amounts of loose change lying around the house. Later on, neighbourhood milk money. I've always been resourceful.

At one stage of my early teen years I had accumulated over $100 in the bank. During one Christmas holidays I got to know bank staff well, as I managed to wipe it out with withdrawals, sometimes twice a day.

Stacking shelves at Woolies a couple of days a week after school, during high school years, provided more economic independence, but a mate and I found a way to increase that. Each Friday morning at school Richard and I had regular customers for the carton of cigarettes we'd helped ourselves to the previous day.

One day Richard and I wagged school, spending the day in the city playing pool, before going to Woolies in the afternoon. On this particular day Richard surprised me. 'We should stop. Sooner or later we'll get caught,' he said. 'Don't be stupid,' I replied, 'this is easy money.'

But he convinced me. That afternoon, as we were leaving Woolies, the manager checked our bags; something that had never happened before. I think Richard had a tip-off. I've occasionally wondered what he would have done if I'd stuck to my guns and not been convinced to stop.

On leaving school I started work with the Commercial Bank of Australia. From a young and impressionable age I had responsibility for handling unimaginably large amounts of cash. Profligacy was in my DNA, but the bank failed its duty of care to me. As it did to many others, staff and customers.

At one branch, soon after completing the probation period, I had duties as an occasional teller, only serving customers with their deposits and withdrawals when the two regular tellers were busy. I didn't have an individual teller's box, as was the custom then, using only a bench cupboard with a sliding door.

This was a very busy branch. When it was very, very busy one – or sometimes two – of the other staff would come and serve customers, using the cash I was responsible for. Full responsibility, without full control.

The bank's policy then was that if there was a shortfall of up to $20 in a teller's cash the bank would cop the loss, with the incident noted against the teller. If the shortfall was $20 or more there was a standard procedure to be followed. It started with a letter addressed to the state manager. A letter I recall well;

> Dear Sir
>
> I regret to inform you that the cash under my control at the close of business on *what-ever-date* revealed a shortfall of *what-ever-it-was* ...

The bank's standard policy was to write back noting that the teller would be required to contribute ten per cent of the loss at the rate of two dollars per fortnightly pay. Now this was a busy branch, there were lots of hands into the cash I was responsible for, and I wrote lots of those letters. All those amounts of two dollars add up.

The largest shortfall, one busy Friday, was $200. First thing next Monday morning the regional manager was waiting for me in the branch manager's office. There was little discussion before I was told I was being transferred to a quieter branch. I don't think I was asked how these losses could have happened, but I'm quite certain that, had I been, I wouldn't have been able to point out this was a case of full responsibility without full control. Such was my level of self-confidence.

The manager, sitting there along-side the regional manager, had been one of the other staff who occasionally served customers with my cash, and he'd been good to me. Less good to me, had been the assistant manager, given to a punt and a boozy lunch. Who very frequently served customers with the cash I was responsible for.

This was outrageous behaviour by the bank, which I accepted. I was 18 and the chip on my shoulder was entering a growth phase.

Apart from that experience, I had many valuable life lessons in the bank. I saw and learnt from decent compassionate managers helping people in dire straits. And I saw miserable bastards who put loyalty to the bank and profit before all else.

In 2018 the federal government commenced a Royal Commission into Misconduct in the Banking, Superannuation and Financial Services Industry. I wrote to the commission;

> In 1974 I worked in an Adelaide branch of the Commercial Bank of Australia. At this time Bankcard, the first mass market credit card, was introduced. At that time letters were sent to all bank customers with a trading (cheque) account offering a Bankcard with, from memory, credit limits of $500 or sometimes $1000. These letters were sent to all customers. This included those customers whose cheques were regularly dishonoured for lack of funds.
>
> I thought this odd and asked the manager, whose response I have never forgotten, "It's the interest rates lad. Most of these people will never pay it off and the bank will make millions."
>
> I appreciate this was one manager of one branch of one bank, more than 40 years ago. But I also believe this may speak to the true nature of banking culture. And nothing much may have changed.

I still recall the joy in the manager's voice.

This was the mid 70s, when the bank went through conversion to a computerised system. I noted that if there was damage to the numbers along the bottom of a cheque these were rejected by the computer and had to be entered manually. One of my tasks was the manual processing of these cheques. Didn't take long to work out that when broke, a regular event some days before a payday, I could cash a cheque at the footy club. After first folding and pinching out some of the numbers. Did I say I was resourceful?

In early 1976 I keenly accepted the offer of a transfer to Darwin. While the ravaged city was a pleasant enough shock to my system, the bank itself was something else. This was just over a year after Cyclone Tracy had made a mess of the city. The place was crawling with enterprising locals and tradies from south making a killing in the reconstruction boom. Hours worked by staff were long and demanding. The bank maintained a system of hegemony, where staff accepted with little question that overtime would not normally be paid, though this was not without its resentments.

People tended to think working in a bank was highly paid which was not the case. Still, there were ways of subsidising the really quite meagre pay. Among bank tellers – and not just in the bank I worked for – there was a widespread practice of taking a commission out of money boxes customers were in the habit of leaving to be counted. Just enough for a beer. Or two. But there was honour. Beer money never came from kids' money boxes.

One teller's entrepreneurial creativity reached great heights. Australia bank notes carry the signature of the Governor of the Reserve Bank and the Secretary to the Treasurer. When these signatures change after a short period, which happens occasionally, those bank notes are less common and considered more valuable by collectors. Our teller, Gary, struck an arrangement with a customer, an avid stamp, banknote and coin collector.

Gary would keep an eye out for these notes, particularly those in good condition and hold them until the collector came in. Then he would sell them at a rate determined by the rarity of the note, generally twenty per cent above the face value. Cheaper than they would have been available elsewhere, the customer thought it was a good deal. So creative was this practice, which might be called a victimless misdemeanour, I doubt the bank had ever dreamt up a rule to ban it.

After a couple of years in Darwin, and following a dispute with the manager, the bank informed me I was being transferred back to Adelaide. My then wife and I decided quickly that I would resign and we would stay.

One of the bank's customers whom we had become friendly with had a small business and offered me a job. Office manager, or something, I was called. I didn't really know what they did beyond it being called a mercantile agency. Not until I started with Jim and Vicky did I discover this was code for debt collector.

Jim, it turned out, had more of a drinking problem than I had realised. When their debt collector left – Peter, six foot something and eight stone wringing wet, but with an impressive ability to have buffalo hunters hand over the keys to the four wheel drive he was repossessing – the business barely had the cash to pay him out. Hiring someone else immediately was out of the question. The solution was that Jim would do more of the debt collecting work and the expectation was that I would help out. This was not something I was prepared for, but felt unable to say no. Friends and all that.

I served a few summons on my own, which was no fun. Went with Jim once on a repossession. The car, from down south, had been located at a motel. We met the tow truck-driver, the vehicle was hooked up and towed to the yard where it was to be stored, with us following. Here, the tow truck driver said he had noticed the curtains move in the unit as he was leaving.

The car's owner, who we later learned was wanted on charges of assaulting police, had been watching from inside. I was pleased he stayed there.

Later that day the car was taken from the street outside the yard where it was to be stored. The owner, cunningly, had noted the name of the tow truck business, then got out there and repossessed his repossessed car.

In 1978 the Commonwealth Government granted self-government to the Northern Territory. This came with costs as the level of Commonwealth subsidies was reduced. One of the most noticeable impacts was a rise in the annual cost of a driver's licence from something like 25 cents to something starting with a dollar sign. To ease that burden, encourage more permanent or longer lasting settlement in what was a largely transient population, and to celebrate self-government, the territory government introduced a home purchase scheme with as little as $1,000 deposit. At this time we were renting a government house. My parents lent us about $700 and we became home owners.

As we had inherited a garden with a lawn, a lawn mower was needed. Money was short, with a wife and one very young child, so I started lawn mowing after work or on weekends, first with a borrowed mower, until I could afford to buy one.

I wasn't happy in my job and looked to increase the number of lawn-mowing customers. What I also craved was control. Not having to work for a boss. The break came when I got a job with a caravan park, a weekly cut at around $110 a week. With a few other jobs this was enough to get by. This was all good until I quit and turned up for the first week at the caravan park, when the manager told me the owner had vetoed her decision. I was to be on an as required basis during the dry season, and weekly only when the wet season arrived and grass started growing. That was still a couple of months away. It could have been a problem but we got by.

Over time I started getting government work: grass cutting, tree lopping and other maintenance jobs on various government properties. The government always paid at the end of the month following that in which the work was done. This sometimes meant a wait of almost two months, but it was reliable. They always paid.

During this time the bank account often went overdrawn towards the end of the month. One time, after some major purchases this was almost $2,000. Not a small amount in the early 1980s. Occasionally the bank would call, just checking the overdrawn amount would be cleared at the end of the month. Never a problem.

After we separated, my wife went to the bank and, quite reasonably, opened an account in her own name, telling them we had separated. Following that, as soon as the joint account went overdrawn – with a cheque of around $20 – the bank dishonoured it. No phone call to say things had changed and they wouldn't be able to continue providing the unsecured overdraft. They just bounced the cheque. This was my personal experience of bank manager as miserable bastard.

When the marriage finally ended I was left with a financial mess. Our taxation arrangements, orchestrated by an accountant and all perfectly legal, had seen 90 per cent of income go into one of our names one year, and the other the next year. This year it was due to go in her name. But she opted out of this arrangement for reasons I can only guess at. I copped a major bill, which I declined to pay. A little later I received a tax office letter advising I was being charged interest of something over five dollars a week. That led to a further deterioration of my attitude. I didn't lodge a return for about six years. When deciding to opt out of annual tax returns I knew that, sooner or later, I would have to return to the system. But I did it anyway. Earlier I mentioned my habit of making decisions that, deep down, I knew wouldn't end well.

There were other expenses I felt I shouldn't have been left with, though no doubt my former wife saw it differently. She may have been more right than me. And while I wasn't able or willing to reign in my spending, bills were accumulating. This led to some unfriendly letters. I saw no point in opening those with a window face. Bad news lay within.

The experience of working for the debt collector had me in good stead. I knew how they worked and used that to advantage. One night when I was house sharing, I had just got into my car, parked close to the front door but in darkness, when a car pulled up on the street. In the rear view mirror I watched a man, paperwork in hand, approach the house. I lay across the bench seat, well out of sight, as my house mate Len answered the knock on the door.

Some summons' have to be served directly on the person named. Others can be left at the address where the person lives. Len knew the drill. The exchange went something like this;

Graeme Gibson?
He doesn't live here anymore.
Are you sure? He was here very recently.
He doesn't live here now.
Where is he now?
Don't know.

Then, after a lengthy pause;

Are you Graeme Gibson?
No mate.

After selling the business I managed the occasional government job, through a friendly contact or two in one or other of the departments I had previously worked for on a regular basis. These jobs I invoiced in the name of C Ash. Colin, Chris, Christine or whoever you like. Cheques came addressed to C Ash at a post office box. I had fantasies of a typo in the cheque production and it being made out to Cash. Never happened but I found it entertaining. The publican saw no problem in cashing these cheques for me.

In 1988, the bicentennial year, the federal government announced a taxation amnesty. I took a deep breath, found an accountant, and lodged multiple year returns. I expected and was prepared for a major bill, but got a refund of nearly $5,000. A reward for my virtue.

Living with uncertainty, financial and other, had become second nature. Meg and I got together in 1992. Her less ambivalent attitude to money, or more specifically debt, helped my attitude change. Being financially responsible, and literate, is part of growing up. Despite the occasional impulse, I'm pleased to say I might be there.

When we moved from Canberra to Huskisson on the NSW south coast in 2000, I got a reminder that some things never leave you. While living in a flat above a shop in the main street of Richmond, in western Sydney, in the mid 1980s, I often copped a parking ticket. There was nowhere near at hand to park. Over a year or so there must have been a few dozen which I didn't pay. When transferring a drivers' licence back to NSW from the ACT the computer system threw up three of these outstanding fines. Only three. I paid without question and got the hell out of there.

Much later on, with the aim of waving goodbye to the mortgage, we sub-divided a block at Huskisson, sold the existing house and built on the 'new' block. We achieved this without a real project budget, other than a few back-of-the-envelope scratchings, along with an attitude that we could pull it off. After initially denying any more money to finish the work, when we ran short, the bank saw reason and allowed us to achieve a win-win. They got all of their money, with their usual interest rate and a minimum of fuss, and we got rid of the mortgage.

PART THREE

Lessons Well Learnt

A man must consider what rich realm he abdicates when he becomes a conformist.

Ralph Waldo Emerson

.

On a good day

Most of the really valuable stuff we learn in life doesn't take place in school, probably not anywhere in the education system, though I learnt some valuable things during post-school study. This came well after school, which I had found largely uninspiring. Time and space after school allowed a desire to learn, to understand, to take root. Underpinning this quest for learning was a stronger drive still – the need to take control, to be steering the ship, even if I didn't know exactly where it was headed.

I have developed a world view from a humanist perspective, with a strong green left slant. I have learnt to take risks: better to go down the wrong street than stand on the corner. I have learnt how bureaucracies work, how to spot incompetence and deceit. I have learnt not to be cowed by authority and to stand up to bullies. I have learnt to ask questions and not take cant for an answer.

On a good day I know what I don't know.

This part of the book is about how I overcame my dismal schooling and equally dismal early years in the workforce, and managed to have a varied working life of mostly self-employment. I was able to dip in and out of various fields, get a feel for whatever it was about, and move on to something else. A chequered approach to a career, but it suited.

The pieces are chronological in the sense that it opens with a couple of experiences of long ago, and closes with much more recent experiences. But it is much more thematic, the various pieces have some common connective threads. In the early pieces, for example, I was able to learn something about myself and what I needed, arising from a smart-arse response to authority. And I was able to recognise something about the world I had been blissfully unaware of. When it was forcefully pointed out to me. This is not all beer and skittles. These pieces are riddled with difficult moments and events, but luckily I have thick skin and can take a philosophical view of these. I have come to see this response as a gift. Not everyone has it but everyone can work at developing it.

And I take joy out of thinking things through. 'Getting a think up,' Meg calls it. I have found connections between many things. Cause and effect. Chaos theory tells us that a small change in one part of a system can lead to large changes in another part of a system. A butterfly flapping its wings in the Amazon is said to create tiny changes in the atmosphere leading to a storm far away. If my life has been a system, from the time I took control, the butterfly has occasionally flapped well, the chaos has been more favourable than not.

Along the way I had some useful lessons, as everyone does. The best of these lessons have been transferable and adhesive. They apply widely and they have stuck well.

Pulling rank

Within a story, dialogue between characters allows a reader to experience events as if they were present, or as if it had happened to them. Dialogue gives a sense of events unfolding. It can make explicit those important things that risk being overlooked. Dialogue moves action forward, revealing a character's mood, emotion, status and more.

In the first piece here the re-created dialogue with Barry, my contract supervisor, shows an escalation of seriousness. And in the second piece the dialogue with Telstra's Karen makes clear the absurdity of the situation.

1. In Part Two I described how I started a gardening and lawn mowing business in Darwin.

When you have regular customers for this sort of work, sooner or later someone will want something else done. Such as planting a tree or making a path. And this is when you become a landscaper, which is how it happened for me.

I started to learn about the natural world at this time. In Darwin a lot of time was spent mowing (mainly in the wet season) and, with some contracts, a lot of time spent watering (mainly in the dry season). I paid close attention to different areas, considering soil, exposure and the balance between sunlight and shade trying to work out how much water was needed to keep grass green enough for the customer to be satisfied, while minimising the extent to which the grass grew, and hence minimising the amount of time needed for mowing. Nothing like self-interest.

At one site, a new government office block on rock hard soil, new lawns and gardens struggled. I learnt something here about gardening, but much more than that. The planting included several weeping, or long leaved paperbarks, *Melaleuca leucadendra*. This attractive tall tree grows naturally on riverbanks, lagoons and low-lying wet areas. But it's adaptable and commonly planted as an ornamental tree in urban parks and gardens. Here though, on super hard soils, they were all struggling.

I was usually at this site at least a couple of times a week and the fellow in charge of the building and the grounds came out regularly for a chat. I had done some work for Barry in his immaculate home garden. To Barry's mind the paperbark's struggle was due, at least in part, to the presence of scale insects on the leaves. These are small, hard-shelled sap suckers. To my mind, they were in quite low numbers and doing little damage.

Our conversation, over a few weeks, started with something like this;

> Those paperbarks aren't doing well. I think the scale insects are part of the problem, Barry said.
>
> The trees haven't been in long, Barry, and they've been planted in pretty hard soil.

It moved on to something like this;

> Those paperbarks are really struggling Graeme. I think you're going to have to spray the scale. It'll help get the trees moving.
>
> They're a natural thing and I don't think they're causing a problem. It's not like it's a large infestation, I responded.

Leading to this;

> I was down at the nursery the other day, Barry said, and they told me the best insecticide to use.
>
> I don't think you'd find a paperbark tree in the country that didn't have some scale insects on it, Barry.

Something of a stand-off emerged. Barry came out less frequently for a chat, a little more clipped when he did. While I was convinced I was right I was disappointed I had been unable to get Barry to see it my way.

After a time I sensed Barry was about to pull rank on me. I conceded the argument and swallowed my pride. Sort of. Next time I turned up I fiddled around at the back of the ute, took the back pack spray unit over to the tap, and then sprayed the paperbarks. Take that scale insects.

A week or so later Barry appeared: 'Thanks for doing the paperbarks Graeme,' he said, 'they're looking better already.' Unbeknown to Barry, I had sprayed them with water. Just water.

Smart arse to be sure, but this was a turning point. My ego suffered in not being able to explain to Barry why I was right and he was wrong. Eventually it dawned on me that I needed a better understanding of what I was doing. I thought a qualification might help and did a term of a horticulture course at Darwin Community College. This was duller than imaginable. Listening to someone read from a text book can be like that. Despite this, or perhaps because of it, I started thinking more broadly, looking further for opportunities. For exactly what I cannot say, but something was brewing.

Apart from running a small business I also learnt a little about ethics and how the little guy can be used, made the scapegoat. This came through a one-year contract with Darwin City Council to maintain the gardens around the newly opened Casuarina Library. After this period council would take over the maintenance. When my contract expired I stopped work. Council forgot to start. Quite quickly it became a serious mess. In response to a ratepayer complaint the *NT News* ran a page three story in which council said it was the responsibility of a contractor, naming me.

I rang the council and had a meeting with the town clerk who apologised and said they would correct the story in the paper, removing blame from me. They didn't. And then the town clerk didn't return my calls. I was unsure what to do and let it go. This was a mistake. I should have persisted, but it was a lesson well learnt that I've carried through life. I don't accept that sort of behaviour.

2. Sometimes you just can't help but think government and industry services are designed to frustrate people into submission. Dogged persistence is needed to overcome this.

'Your call is important to us,' brings on a number of emotions, none of them positive. 'Don't take this personally,' I have trained myself to say to the call centre staff, most often based in the Philippines or India, 'it's not you I'm cranky with.'

Like many people I had a 'courtesy' call from Telstra, wanting to review our account, to make sure we were getting the best deal, as they say. This was in 2019. Not long before this call, Meg and I had decided we would do some serious shopping around for an alternative provider, so I went through the process with some interest.

A couple of months later we had found a comparable service at half the price, so I called Telstra to make arrangements to cancel our service. Telstra's Karen told me that as our contract had recently been extended there would be a disconnection fee of $536.84 on each of the mobile phones. Now that was a surprise. The conversation went something close to this;

    ME: But I haven't extended the contract.

    KAREN: Let me look it up.

                  [A few minutes pass]

	It was done by voice contract during the review a couple of months back.
ME:	I don't remember being asked to extend the contract and I think I would remember that.
KAREN:	OK, I'll arrange to get a copy of the voice recording that was made. This will tell us whether there was agreement, mis-information or non-agreement; whether the correct procedure was followed. The call was made by TSA, our outbound telemarketing subsidiary and it'll have to come from them. This will take a couple of days and I'll call you then.

Some days later;

KAREN:	My supervisor has listened to the call and at around the 13-minute mark the terms and conditions were read out. The correct procedure was followed, therefore the cancellation fee applies.
ME:	Well, I still don't think I agreed to the extension. I'd like to listen to the recording of the conversation. How do I get that?
KAREN:	The recording isn't available to customers.
ME:	Why not?
KAREN:	For privacy reasons.
ME:	Privacy! This was a call between Telstra and me about our Telstra account. How can there be a privacy issue?
KAREN:	I'll check with my supervisor.
	[Several minutes later]
	No, the recording isn't available to customers. If you want to you can refer it to Telstra's privacy section.

Which, after thanking the amiable Karen, who I suspect recognised how absurd this was, I did, the following day.

A few days on and I had a call from Kristine, a 'Telstra Complaints Resolution Coordinator.' Kristine told me the recording 'can't be provided to customers because it's purpose is for quality and training purposes only.' I asked Kristine to put this information in writing, which she promptly did. Shortly after this a second email came from Kristine;

> I was able to listen to the sales call recording and our sales consultant was able to discussed [sic] the contract for the 2 mobiles on the account and offered to send the Customer Information Summary to the email address you provided within the call. I've consulted our subject matter experts and coaches about sending the call recording and was advised that we don't send it to customers as the purpose of recording the calls is for training and quality purposes only. Please let me know if you need more details.

Is this not a quality matter I wondered? I sensed though, this was futile and emailed Kristine, thanking her for her advice and advising I was lodging a complaint with the Telecommunications Industry Ombudsman (TIO). This is a straight-forward process on-line that generates an automatic acknowledgement with a reference number and an assurance they will be on to it within a few days.

Three days later a letter arrived setting out the process and their aim to have the complaint resolved within two weeks. Interestingly the letter included this statement: 'Most complaints to the TIO are resolved after a service provider receives a complaint from us and contacts their customer.'

And that's exactly what happened.

I had a phone call from Dinesh, a 'Telstra *Complex* Complaints Resolution Coordinator.' Obviously a further rung up the complaints resolution hierarchy than Kristine. Dinesh must have sensed the game was up. In my shortest conversation over this saga he said he knew how the phone consultants rush through so much information and people often have trouble understanding. I'm pretty certain I had no difficulty understanding the information I received, but then again, most people would say that, wouldn't they? And from the way he spoke I suspect he hadn't even bothered to listen to the recording. The good news though, was that the mobile phone contracts would be cancelled immediately.

So that was a good outcome, if an entirely avoidable waste of time.

From Dinesh's comments it's reasonable to believe my complaint is not uncommon. I was confronted by polite but consistent blocking to my request, which may deter some people from continuing with their complaint. But as soon as I go through the TIO – which was a little like pulling rank on Telstra – it all changes.

The TIO lodgement process asks for preferred outcome. I said I would like Telstra to review their interpretation of 'training and quality' so others don't have my frustration. So Telstra can't continue with this shoddy practice. Probably wishful thinking.

I asked Dinesh for a response to this, also what guidance might be provided, or review of the procedures phone consultants follow, to ensure Telstra customers fully understand the information they are receiving. After all, Dinesh identified this as being at the heart of the complaint; a not uncommon complaint. I was told my feedback would be provided to all agents and will be an internal process. The level of complaints to the TIO is rising and Telstra is an over-achiever in this regard.

On dialogue

Writing and speech are different. Writing aims to be very clear, understandable and coherent. On the other hand speech, unless it's reading a script, is very often imprecise, repetitive, fragmented and uses a lot of filler words.

Think twice before using anything other than simple tags or attributions like 'said,' 'asked' or 'replied.' When you say someone whispered or shouted you are implying something about their character, or state of mind. Which you may want to do, but you should be aware of this. Someone who whispers may be shy. Or sneaky. Someone who shouts may be angry. Or hard of hearing and thinks everyone else is. The state of mind, or motive takes on a more prominent role in the story, which you may not want. The neutral attributions should be the default position. Use others with care.

There will be a dilemma from time to time in recording conversations when you don't recall all the details. Or when you weren't there. You might say: 'The conversation went something like this.'

An author note might say: 'Conversations are re-created from my research, as I imagine they occurred,' giving some idea of the research. This may be newspaper records, family history, court records or a local history of your town.

The aim is to re-create conversation, not create. Illuminate, not deceive. Do this with best judgement and good intent. And use neutral attributions.

Direct quotes should be indicated in single quotation marks, while a quote within a quote uses double marks. Indirect quotes should be paraphrased as necessary and do not need quotation marks.

Generally, dialogue should be indented or a space left between paragraphs. Italics may be used so dialogue stands out from other text. In these cases it probably doesn't need quotation marks. And it may be that the dialogue is so crisp that the speaker is clear and attributions are not needed.

What it is to be human

In part one I talked about memoir encapsulating change in the memoir writer: their failures, learning, a transformative inner journey known as a character arc. You were … You have become … The lesson in the following piece about John, a homeless man with a good heart, points to a transformation. In me. This is character arc in extreme brevity.

The first draft of this story started with: 'In 2003 we went on holiday to Fiji.' Which is very ho hum. But that's the first draft, the aim of which is just to get it all down. Once the story is down it can be worked into something readable and worthwhile.

Originality is rare in first drafts. The closing of the first draft here used the cliché: 'There but for the grace of God go I.' This was rewritten as: 'In life there is luck, some good, some not.'

I'm Australian and I'm generally pretty happy about that. I'm happy enough with most other Australians, but when on holiday overseas I don't want to be hanging around with Australians. That's not the purpose of travel. In 2003 while on holiday in Fiji we had been several days on the main island, Viti Levu, when we called in to the tourist office in Suva seeking advice on where we might find somewhere, 'out of the way.'

Vanua Balavu was the answer. An outer island in the far east with a guesthouse and two flights a week, next one being the following day. So off we went with great expectations. From the airport we caught a ride into the main village of Lomaloma, asking to be taken to the guest house. With what seemed a little uncertainty we were dropped at a rather delightful house with rounded roof, typical of this island and its heavy Tongan influence. Turns out the guesthouse the Suva tourist office had in mind had just closed down. But the nephew of the owner of the just-closed-down guesthouse, Tevita Fotofili, and his wife Caroline, had just opened Moana's Guesthouse.

And this is where we had a very special week. We were in fact their second guests, but in the relationship we built up with Tevita and Caroline over the following years they called us the first guests. They hadn't taken to their (strictly speaking) first guests, who had beaten us by one flight.

A couple of years later we were back again, this time for a month, building a bure on their land, a little out of the village and directly on the beach. Their guesthouse business had expanded from the earliest days and they now had three bures. Ours would be built almost entirely in the traditional method, with reed walls and leaf roof. The only modern parts of the building were a concrete floor, sawn timber in the door and window frames and the use of raffia instead of handmade coconut fibre string.

For the locals who would prefer a tin roof, it being much easier to collect water from, this was a little novel. Perhaps a folly only westerners could justify. Nevertheless, it was a great opportunity for some of the older men to use their traditional building skills and show younger ones how it was done. And quite a skilful process it was to observe, and play a small part in the actual building.

Our arrangement with Tevita and Caroline was that we would use it whenever we liked, but for the rest of the time it would be part of the guesthouse and available for their use. All up it cost us less than many people spend on a home theatre system.

The first few day's work were spent clearing the land, weeding and piling up old coconuts for burning. I spent much of this time digging out a particularly deep rooted and persistent shrub or small tree, *Leucaena leucocephala*. In the sandy soil a ten centimetre plant could have a taproot five times that length. A native of central America this legume makes an excellent fodder plant and has been established in many tropical countries where it becomes weedy, often invading large areas. I knew it as coffee bush and knew it well from my time in Darwin. Digging it out on Vanua Balavu, where it is known as *Vaivai*, triggered a memory. A memory far more powerful than woody weed control.

I occasionally had work clearing coffee bush from various areas around the city. It grew dense and tall, often blocking harbour views, which can not be tolerated. One of these jobs was a vacant block on the edge of the city centre.

Deep in this block, and barely visible from the street, was a corrugated iron lean-to, the camp of an old fellow, commonly known around town as Stinker. Most city regulars in those days would have seen Stinker, bustling around town with a collection of dogs he attracted and fed. His camp was strewn with scattered personal belongings, blankets and pieces of clothing along with masses of rubbish, notably polystyrene meat trays and baked bean tins.

I had been contracted by the Department of Lands who had told Stinker the block was to be cleared and given him a date by which he needed to move, taking his possessions. I was to start the following day. Along with clearing the coffee bush, part of the job was to remove the lean-to. My instructions were to remove this and clean up the camp site before removing the coffee bush. Whether intentional or not this would have the effect of keeping the camp site out of public view. I wasn't aware of any arrangements being made for Stinker's future needs. It's likely that at an official level there were none. Perhaps a friend or community agency offered something.

I arrived early on the first day and he was out. It was apparent he hadn't moved his belongings. Stinker turned up later that morning and, with a little remonstration, said he needed more time to move his belongings. All he had worth taking would have fitted into one smallish suitcase.

I started on the coffee bush in the back of the block, removing rubbish as I went. This was particularly unpleasant, being malodorous, to say the least. It became apparent the job was going to be behind schedule and I needed to update my contact in the department, so wandered over the road to the adjacent health department clinic and asked to use their phone. Darwin was pretty casual in those days. The conversation with a woman behind the desk went something like this;

> What are you doing over there?
>
> Moving Stinker's stuff and clearing the block, I replied, before adding, unnecessarily, how unpleasant this job was.
>
> Where's he going to move to? she enquired.
>
> Don't know, don't care.

The response was swift and merciless. I was informed that I didn't know anything about life, other than the need to make a dollar; I had no idea of the difficult circumstances some people found themselves in, through no fault of their own selves; and what an entirely decent and caring man he was, spending his days running errands and caring for older people who lived nearby in public housing. And how dare I call John, Stinker.

Put in my place, I learned something that day. Life is not black and white. In life there is luck, some good, some not. Misfortune lies in wait, trapping many in a cold embrace. And to the woman who educated me, I offer my thanks. You changed my worldview and gave me a lesson in thinking things through, looking beyond the surface, in one brief (if bruising) encounter.

A sense of shame necessarily accompanied that changing worldview, but this was okay. I have moved on. We have all done things that lead us to a sense of shame. And shame applies to countries as well as people.

For much of the time between 1970-75 I lived in Adelaide's Eden Hills. From the beginning I was vaguely aware of a nearby Aboriginal children's home, Colebrook Home. This was where many children who had been forcibly removed from their parents, in what later became known as The Stolen Generation, lived. That some of these children lost all contact with their families and their culture, and had quite brutal experiences is now well known.

At the time though, this was of no interest. Like others in my peer group, I knew no Aboriginal people and had only the deeply flawed teachings from school about Australian Aboriginal people.

In 1976 I went to live in Darwin. Here I became friendly with, and then came to know quite well, an Aboriginal family. The wife and mother of this family, Betty, was originally from somewhere around Alice Springs, possibly northern South Australia. She told me that as a child she had gone – I don't believe she said she was taken, though she may have – to live in Adelaide. Here she lived with a white family, and also in an Aboriginal children's home. What came first I do not know.

Sometime in 1997 I spent a night alone in a motel room in Albury, on the NSW Victorian border. I stayed up late, poring over *Bringing them home*, the report of the Inquiry into the Stolen Generation of Aboriginal children. I read of the impacts of forced removal on children and their parents. I learned of the inter-generational trauma and on-going impacts. These were horrendous and I don't accept the 'it was for their own good' rhetoric and the associated spin that goes with it. Or, 'they should just get over it.'

While in Darwin, during my friendship with the Aboriginal family, I observed, and later came to understand better, some of the difficulties of this family. Difficulties which led to the early deaths of two of its men. And I think some of the families' difficulties may be attributable to Betty's early years, about which *Bringing them home* has this to say;

> Most forcibly removed children were denied the experience of being parented or at least cared for by a person to whom they were attached. This is the very experience people rely on to become effective and successful parents themselves. Experts told the Inquiry that this was the most significant of all the major consequence of the removal policies.

There were other Aboriginal children's homes and orphanages in Adelaide but occasionally I wonder if Betty had been at the Eden Hills home. If this had been the case, it would have been before I lived in the area. Even so, I wonder.

I was parented and cared for by my natural parents. Though all my material needs were met and there was no abuse, from my birth family I developed few skills to guide the development of the most personal of relationships, with a family of one's own. I have asked myself if I use this as cover for my own failings. Truth is I'm too close to know.

But if the circumstances of my upbringing acted as a deadweight on my situation some years later, I have no difficulty in seeing how Betty's experience may have set the course of her life. And a lot of people shared Betty's experience.

And then there was Mitchell, a team mate from the footy club. Mitchell and I were useful B-graders, about the same age, but there the similarities end, he being a teetotal churchgoer. Mitchell was quite fair skinned, little darker than I after a few years outside in the Territory sun, and I had not realised he was part Aboriginal until one night at a footy club barbeque.

A small group of us were talking about whatever you talk about while waiting for the weekend teams to be announced when something Mitchell said made me ask what he meant.

'My mother was a native on Wave Hill,' he replied, as my penny started its slow descent. And that's when he spoke his life's history. Or its void. Mitchell had grown up in a church mission on an island north of Darwin, while his 'mother was a native on Wave Hill,' 750 kilometres from Darwin.

Mitchell's mother may have been dead, which would warrant the past tense. But whether past or present tense, if his mother was a native, where exactly, does Mitchell see himself in the scheme of things. Did he ever wonder, I wonder?

All countries have chapters in their past, sometimes their present, deserving of an apology, reparation. Including Australia. And there is a world of difference between being sorry for past events and being responsible for them. Sorry, and an apology, does not equal responsibility and guilt. That former Prime Minister John Howard could continually spout that deceit while keeping a straight face is a feat only a leaden heart could maintain. That it took until a change of government in 2008 for a national apology to the Stolen Generations is a national shame. A further national apology followed in 2009 to the more than 500,000 children and child migrants who had been placed into institutional care, with many suffering abuse and neglect.

The time will come when there is a national apology to refugees and asylum seekers over the cruel and inhuman treatment they have received over many years. But with both major political parties being equally culpable this seems years away.

Working to one's strengths?

After leaving Darwin for Cairns I had some work in the horticultural area. Firstly, a nursery, from where I was sacked for insolence towards the owner's wife. I wasn't cut out to be a servant. After this a short stint with Cairns City Council was an eye-opener. As a casual I wasn't awarded the orange vest that permanent gardening staff wore and stashed in the shrubbery somewhere, before a beer at 10am and another at 2pm. Wasn't a busy job. It gave me more impetus to think about what I wanted, which wasn't what I had. This was a turning point where I started to take control, making my own luck.

When I was almost 30 I moved from Cairns to western Sydney to start a two-year full- time course in horticulture at Hawkesbury Agricultural College. I made my first enquiry on the day the academic year had started. Fortuitously I spoke with a staff member who had a view that students, or potential students, should have things made easy for them. We spoke several times over a week before he gave me a deadline of one more week, if I wanted to enrol. I was disheartened in Cairns but still pondered the decision long and hard before deciding to do it. Better to go down the wrong street than stand on the corner.

Arriving at the horticulture section of the college on the morning of the deadline I discovered my helpful staff member wasn't in and he had forgotten to tell anyone else of the special arrangement he had made with me. It was eventually sorted out.

I hadn't much experience of any formal learning since leaving school and I wasn't good in group situations, of which there were many at Hawkesbury. One night at a local pub, one of the academic staff gave me some of the best advice I have ever received. Many people freeze at participation in group discussions, particularly in large groups. I wasn't paralysed but I wasn't particularly confident either. The advice was, when the opportunity to participate comes – either question or comment – be the first to speak. Even if to ask a question you know the answer to, be the first. When you do this, when you hear your own voice, everything becomes easier. And if you aren't first to speak, make certain you are second. After this, it gets harder and harder to speak. At which point it's easier to say nothing and hope you get through unnoticed. I have passed this advice on to many others over the years since.

Unlike anything else I had experienced, education at Hawkesbury was based on systems thinking. This is a holistic approach that focuses on the way the various pieces of a system interrelate, how they work over time and as part of a larger system. Think of a natural system where plants are dependent on soil for providing nutrients, water and support. Soil is dependent on plants whose ultimate decomposition enriches the soil. And so it goes. All things within a system are connected, even when the connections are unclear. A similar pattern of connections applies to human activities. This took about a year and a half to fully sink in, but it's been fundamental to my thinking ever since.

At least within a horticultural context there is a clear distinction between the systems thinking approach (such as at Hawkesbury) and a more vocational approach (such as at TAFE). The focus at Hawkesbury was on learning how to think, to solve problems. The focus at TAFE was on learning about plants. The horticultural industry, at that time, largely preferred TAFE graduates.

Alongside occasional landscaping jobs, and working in a pub, I got work teaching a home gardening course at Penrith Evening College. I don't think the class members got great value for their money, but it was important to me. More important than I realised at the time.

Horticulture at Hawkesbury was two years of technical subjects. The grading here was Unsatisfactory, Satisfactory, Credit, Distinction. At the completion of two years I received a grading of Satisfactory in all subjects. Excellence in mediocrity you might say. When I tell people I'm a horticulturist, I have often added, 'but I'm not a very good one.' As I write this it occurs to me perhaps I should be saying 'I'm a satisfactory one,' or, 'a thinking one.'

After Hawkesbury I completed a Graduate Diploma in Environmental Management which was a mix of physical science and sociological subjects. I fared badly in the physical sciences and did well in the sociological area. Following this I completed a Masters in Environmental Education. This was entirely educational or sociological subjects. I did very well.

The take home message was that the sociological area – or soft science, with a people focus – suits me well. This has become a strength. The technological or hard science area is hard work, and best left to others, and I am pleased there are people who excel in this. Perhaps the level of perceived relevance was the major indicator. If I'm being honest, the purpose of memoir after all, there may be an element of laziness here. And the dye may have been set years earlier, in high school.

Back then, in South Australia, there were seven years of primary school followed by five years of high school. In first year of high school I studied maths 1 and 2 and was graded A's. In second year I again did maths 1 and 2 but slipped to D's. In third year I was relegated to maths 3 and again received a D. Meg, who studied to be a maths teacher (and I never thought I'd happily live with one of them), says some foundation concept didn't get through and no one picked it up. In fourth year I was down to maths 4, described in brackets as, 'Arithmetic.' The ship was steady at a D, and when I repeated fourth year the anchor was fast. Another D. Still, I'm handy at arithmetic, rarely resorting to a calculator.

And, to the joy of the teacher, I dropped out of chemistry. The chemistry teacher doubled as the A grade football coach and I was a B grader, which possibly added to his joy. I didn't go on to fifth year, or matriculation. School provided no inspiration that I recall. On leaving I remember thinking, and it's possible I even said it out loud: 'That's the end of this learning for me.'

How the world changes.

My brilliant career takes off

After Hawkesbury I worked for a couple of years with TAFE in western Sydney as a casual horticulture or landscaping teacher, mainly on labour market programs for unemployed people. Many of the programs I worked on were with young people, and many of these young people had no relationship with, or no role models of, people in employment. This was the late 1980s. My TAFE work evolved a little, into coordinating programs in unrelated area, such as retail skills and home support.

Self-employment had taught me good organisational skills which I applied here, having more fun than I could have expected. Leading a group of women in a return to work course on visits to potential employers was a great experience. I learnt something about cultural differences as well, being the only male among groups of women from many different countries. This was a different direction from working as a landscaper and opened my eyes to a world of possibilities and a world of things I was capable of. Thank you, Penrith Evening College.

Later I got a job with the high title of landscape manager at Lizard Island working for the tourist resort. This was the most northerly resort on the Great Barrier Reef and I had what I thought was the most interesting horticultural job on the reef. Whereas every other horticultural job focused on growing traditional ornamental plants – think hibiscus, bougainvillea – my work was based on propagating native plants growing on the island to replace the traditional ornamentals which did very poorly or were at risk of becoming invasive in the national park. No-one else was doing this in the late 1980s.

Eighteen months of island life was enough for me and I moved to the NSW north coast where I hung around for a few months, without getting anything permanent or satisfying, and then landed a job with Greening Australia, based in Brisbane. This was the beginning of the One Billion Trees program, initiated by the federal Labor government. The program had its launch, in the first month of my starting, in a south-western Brisbane suburb. The launch site, which became known (at least for a while) as One Billion Trees Park was perfect. It was a fairly desolate park adjacent to a school that wanted to be involved in tree planting and associated nature study in the park. And it was in a Labor seat.

The launch involved 1,000 school kids, bussed in from around the district, planting 1,000 trees on a Friday morning. Along with the kids Hazel Hawke as patron of Greening Australia was there, as was Graham Richardson, then Minister for the Environment. And then came the media, with television cameras up a cherry picker (this was pre-drone), the police and whoever qualified as a dignitary in those parts. I got my first close look at how the media operated in this intensely planned promotional exercise.

Hazel, full of charm, spoke to the kids, telling them how important this was, before finishing her speech with, 'let's go and get stuck in.' These were little kids, planting little plants in big holes needing to be back filled with big soil. This was some of the heaviest clay soil in Queensland, with clumps the size of a football making the task onerous. Or worse. A great deal of re-planting was needed throughout the rest of that day.

During the morning a newspaper reporter asked how many zeros there were in one billion. Good question. People looked the other way or pretended not to hear before someone came up with the answer, nine. It's a British billion; 1,000,000,000, or one thousand million, not an American or European billion, which is 1,000,000,000,000, or one million million.

By the following Monday about 70 of the trees were dead. Some had been missed during the initial follow-up watering and not survived a few dry Queensland summer days. A simple mistake easily made. The majority of the 70 odd, had been vandalised and the future looked grim. But from that Monday on the school got actively involved with maintenance and monitoring of the planting and there was very little ongoing vandalism. That's a lesson in ownership.

The lesson continued some years later when I was back in Brisbane and decided to check in on One Billion Trees Park. Things had changed. It was apparent that love and care of the park had lapsed. It was now somewhat overgrown and in a sad way. Which is what happens when a project is reliant on too few people.

At Greening Australia I had an education position primarily to work with school kids. The position came with a fair degree of autonomy and I quickly worked out that working with school kids wasn't going to get far, and didn't excite me. The need was to work with teachers who worked with kids. And while planting trees in a school ground is admirable, it's also limited and there was much to be gained by linking schools with other community projects.

The One Billion Trees program dovetailed with the launch of the much larger Decade of Landcare and the National Landcare Program. This was the result of combined lobbying from the National Farmer's Federation and the Australian Conservation Foundation, both headed by quite strong and visionary characters, able to get their respective organisations collaborating rather than opposing each other, as had been the norm. These were inspiring times.

Thirty years on it seems almost impossible to imagine this happening today. While farmers and environmentalists have sometimes combined to oppose mining or other developments, for the most part they have re-grouped into their tribes, back in opposition to each other. Mistrust and misunderstanding chart the course.

With the autonomy the position came with I could do pretty much as I wished and took a great deal of interest in the drier inland areas, where tree planting was largely seen as something to shade the back porch or a corner of the stock yard and little else. I was not welcomed everywhere I went, but to make up for the lack of welcome I was well scrutinised.

At a pub in central Queensland early one evening the barman told me I should leave. Now. I hadn't noticed the looks coming in my direction from some station workers further down the bar. This was a time when few knew the difference between Greenpeace (dangerously radical, in the news) and Greening Australia (conservative, in the background) and even less seemed to care. To be a Green was asking for it.

I enjoyed the challenge of breaking down the resistance, though not always in the front bar. Asking people what they knew about Greening Australia was my starting strategy. Few had any of their facts straight. When they get the facts it can change their views. Sometimes, but not reliably. Even when it doesn't, no harm can come from a civil conversation.

The approach of the Landcare program which had started at the same time moved away from one-on-one extension, where a government agriculture or soil conservation employee provided recommendations, to a supported but self-managing group making their own decisions. My interest in adult education was growing and I learned a lot from watching how others worked with groups, and tried to put it into practice. Over time I became more effective.

After a couple of years, feeling disillusioned with Brisbane, and not quite fitting in, I started planning a move back north. Tree planting was fashionable around Cairns and the wet tropics, less so around Townsville. I was mounting a case in my head for a new position there, in the dry tropics. Going against the flow was often my way.

Quite unexpectedly, late in 1992, I got a better offer in Canberra. A personal offer which I accepted whole heartedly. I moved south, not north. My last month was spent with a lot of travel, often to places where I had been an occasional or regular visitor. The response I received to news of my moving to Canberra was predictable. After all, 'In Canberra today …' is where much of the daily bad news comes from.

Soon after arrival in Canberra, during a recession with unemployment high and rising, I took myself off at the appointed time to the local

TAFE College, seeking part-time teaching hours. I walked out a couple of hours later with a 12-month contract position as full-time coordinator of a youth labour market program: the Landcare and Environment Action Program (LEAP). 'Someone should tell him there's a recession,' one of my new Canberra friends was heard to say.

During the year I started the post-graduate program in environmental education. This involved a research component which became my work with LEAP program participants who were 15 to 20 years of age. I enjoyed working with the young people and combining it with my research, though I found the TAFE structure quite burdensome. After 12 months I didn't seek a contract extension, concentrating on part-time teaching and my research.

The methodology I used is called 'action research'. This is a rigorous cycle of planning, acting, reflecting and then, with adjustment as necessary, doing it again. In simple terms I think of it as 'make it up as you go along'. Suited me well.

Environmental education in those days had three components. Education *in* the environment is about outdoor education, perhaps providing opportunities to connect with nature. Education *about* the environment is the transfer of information, think geography and the natural sciences. Education *for* the environment aims to develop interest and concern for environmental conservation, with associated behaviours, attitudes and values.

You can't develop positive behaviours, attitudes and values towards the environment without wondering why others may have different responses. Understanding those different responses takes you into the realm of critical thinking and the development of political literacy.

For these reasons education *for* the environment was unpopular with conservative educational views that prefer the straight transfer of knowledge. Industry, who often liked to sponsor environmental projects as a public relations exercise, were also critical. It was here, however, that I believed lies the greatest opportunity for positive change.

It's a truism that governments of all persuasions believe that unemployed people should be put to work on environmental projects: tree planting, weed control on riverbanks, walking tracks in nature parks and the like. My experience, which went way beyond this period of working with unemployed youth, was that most enjoyed the routine, the work, being part of a team that was doing something positive. Despite this the majority of the participants, and research has shown this to be consistently around two thirds, did not aspire to working in the environmental field.

If the skills development component of these programs is weighted too heavily on the side of correct methods of tree planting, weed control and walking track construction, for example, then we do the participants a disservice. We sell them short.

Critical thinking includes knowing how to interrogate and interpret information, and to identify what information might be irrelevant, or missing from different options. Political literacy requires an understanding of how government works and of important issues facing society.

Occasionally an opportunity arises to try something extraordinary and this came to Canberra in January 1995. The forest industry, having been in a state of dismay over federal policies for several months, blockaded Parliament House. The LEAP team I had been working with had been interested in the issue of forest management: jobs, conservation, the whole thing. It was all over the news and I raised the prospect of visiting Parliament House with the team.

We talked at length about the emotions people might be feeling and how to deal with the confrontation that might arise. We had often talked about stereotypes, which may have helped when I drew their attention to the obvious. Their age, physical appearance and dress may contribute to a perception they were opposed to logging. But they were keen, and off we went, well prepared.

A few sneers and jeers made the experience quite uncomfortable without ever feeling threatening, after all this was Australia, where outsiders don't generally get beaten up in broad daylight. We wandered for some time through a sea of checked flannelette and big beards, seeking someone in some sort of leadership role hoping to find a useful conversation. This finally came with a remarkable woman from Gippsland, who was able to participate in a two-way conversation with the team. As the conversation started, she was ringed by a group of men, scowling deeply. Reinforcement if needed. This woman had her views, but she knew how to listen. The team were also quite remarkable in their ability to respectfully question the information she presented. I took only a minor role.

I like to think Gippsland woman learnt something that day. I know the team found a deep level of understanding from the exchange. We debriefed the whole experience extensively and, as I write, 25 years on, I reckon those young people will remember their visit to Parliament House. I managed a few other memorable times and felt entirely validated in the approach I had been working on. Mass culture with its consumption habits is the antithesis of an environmentally, socially and economically sustainable world. Critical thinking can help to change that.

There is a world of difference between aiming to develop political literacy and aiming to indoctrinate with a particular political view. The trouble is, when you mention political literacy, there are those who will scream blue-murder and green brain-washing. She who shouts loudest and first sets the agenda. A nuanced rebuttal plays catch-up as the wagon moves on.

There is also a long-held and deep-seated belief among educators and others that if you educate children on environmental matters, they will educate their parents. A sort of trickle-up approach. But while this has been the guiding light for environmental education for decades, the state of the environment in Australia has, in most regards, steadily declined. Trickle-up on its own doesn't work. Education is essential, but a reversal of the long downward spiral the planet is on needs complimentary legislation.

I found influences on my developing methods from widely disparate sources. In his work with illiterate slum dwellers, Brazilian educator and philosopher Paulo Freire aimed to achieve 'conscientization,' a process of perceiving social, political and economic contradictions. Within my outlook this was entirely relevant for unemployed young people in wealthy and developed Australia.

At an entirely different level, American educator Ira Shor described the 'institutional personalities' that develop in many young people. These manifest in passive resistance with non-attendance, non-performance and blank agreement. Active resistance includes vandalism, fighting and challenges to authority. This was, still is, the experience of many young people to the Australian education system.

In Part One I talked about the possibility of viewing life through a sociological lens to present a broader context. I have done this several times throughout this previous piece. For instance, noting that many young people in the late 1980s were not well acquainted with other people in regular employment might make someone wonder how much that has changed in the 30 plus years since. And what that may mean for the overall society. The almost wistful recollection of what is possible when leaders of good will move beyond their political tribes might provoke some thought on the relentless negativity now so regularly shown by leaders as a matter of course. The continuing culture wars and the widespread reflexive disdain for Canberra, seen by many as the source of little that is good, translates into disengagement and a loss of ability or willingness to reason.

On descriptive detail

> A good writer describes everything. A great writer only describes what is necessary.
>
> **Anonymous**

Thick, or detailed description will likely overload the reader, while thin, or scant description, will risk confusion. The anonymous advice presents a common conundrum, a matter of judgement to ponder. In writing about the experience with the timber industry I spent a lot of time re-living the visit to Parliament House, recalling the atmosphere, focusing on small details. A 'sea of checked flannelette and big beards' is memorably visual and captures this, as does 'a group of men scowling deeply.' This is aided by the slightly uncommon but absolutely appropriate verb that is scowling.

Follow your instinct. What comes to mind first, is very often best. As a default position though, err on the side of understatement rather than explaining everything, risking burial by detail. Readers' have experience, instinct and imagination. Respect this and invite them to use it. Every detail must earn its place. Less is more.

Nouns and verbs are the vital ingredients, the main course that satisfies most, while adjectives and adverbs are the condiments that offer a little extra flavour. Make the verb do the work. These are the doing words, the actions that bring life to stories. Be precise with your nouns: the names of people, things, places, ideas or actions. Was it a bird, or a fairy wren? Was it an old car, or an EH Holden?

Choose adjectives with care. It is far better to find one adjective that provides the effect you are after rather than a string of adjectives. Even better if the adjective you use is a little uncommon.

Question the adverb, the great modifier. Why walk slowly when you can amble, or saunter? And wouldn't you rather someone bolted, than ran quickly? The point is if you need to modify your verb you may have the wrong verb.

Use your thesaurus, but use your imagination more. Metaphor, simile, imagery and association can paint a picture. Be plain and direct, specific not vague, vivid and lively. Did the transport system break down? Or was the bus late? Have you had a dream? Or are you working on a vision statement.

I've written most of this book in the princess room. A medium-sized room in a medium-sized house. Built around 1910 for one of the managers of one of the local timber mills it made the most of the local resource. Timber floors, walls and ceilings, with the walls being 12-foot high (or 3.6 metres) for air flow in a sub-tropical climate. To modernise the airflow a ceiling fan whirrs away overhead as needed, such as today when it's 37.

A sash window off to one side uses a stick as prop and two French doors open to a verandah where a grape vine protects from the afternoon sun, which being west facing can be quite brutal. The vine presents more grapes than we can manage. Plenty left for the nightly fruit bats and the day time king parrots with their inquisitive gaze. The princess room is entered through a doorway from the hall, permanently open except when I'm up early and not wanting to disturb my sleeping companion in an adjacent room.

In this room I sit on a fit ball, which for a long stint is kinder to my back than a chair. I sit at an old silky oak desk which faces the French doors and offers plenty of distraction. A printer sits within a narrow but tall hutch cupboard which I occasionally stand at for variety. As I am doing now. This faces a wall with limited distraction potential. Perhaps my productivity rises here.

Some see it as a messy, over-crowded room. They point to the over-flowing book shelves and piles of papers and books on the floor, or any available flat surface. Such as a three-seater lounge, converting to a bed, though barely recognisable as a three-seater lounge.

Above an eight-inch (200 mm) skirting board the walls are painted pink to the eight foot mark. From the ceiling down they are painted lilac. At the point where the two colours meet, a strip of wallpaper, eight inches wide, runs around all walls. The wallpaper print is of flowers and young girls with wings in flouncy dresses. All lilac and pink, of course.

The rest of the house is painted a sickly shade of yellow. Only this room has had the special treatment. Clearly a princess once occupied this room. And now, as occupant of the room, I am the princess. The keeper of the story of the room. A room that, like the rest of the house, will be painted soon. But to preserve the heritage, the story, a small strip of these colours and the wall paper, around 15 inches wide will be kept from floor to ceiling. To honour the previous princess.

Finding a niche

'Whatever you do don't say that in your graduation interview,' was advice I received from one of the friendly staff towards the end of my two years at Hawkesbury. I had responded to a question about what I was going to do after the course finished with something like: 'Well I think I'm unemployable. I wouldn't hire me, so I'll have to work for myself.' As I have, for the greater extent of my working life.

On finishing the full-time role at TAFE in Canberra, and while seeking contract work in the development of community education programs, I had the opportunity to focus on areas of interest for professional development.

In her role with the ACT Parks Service, Meg had a week's training in facilitation processes. Facilitation is about working with a group to make their task easy, to help them reach their goals. A facilitator is much more a guide than a teacher. She came home with a yellow folder full of different ideas. I didn't exactly purloin the folder – I always gave it back when it was asked for – but I found a world full of different methods of working with groups of people to be quite fascinating.

Strategic Questioning, developed by an American social justice and environmental activist and educator named Fran Peavey, was one of these. Peavey's approach to facilitating change used questions that create options, momentum and go beyond the superficial. They are open questions that cannot be answered yes or no. And they avoid asking why, which often leads to a defensive response, more justification than enquiry. Strategic Questioning comes in two levels, with the first crystallising the issue or problem to be addressed. This is about what is known. The second level is transformative and goes from what is known to what could be. Having long believed in questioning the orthodoxies, taking a sceptical approach, this was exciting. It provided a structure for my beliefs.

A sceptic questions the givens in society and takes on new information with an approach that it may be valid, but needs to be interrogated, or at least parked in a holding bay before being accepted. A cynic starts from a default position of doubting the sincerity of people's benevolence and tends to believe actions are based on self-interest. Scepticism, which accommodates uncertainty and helps refine thought processes, is good: cynicism, which claims the truth and closes down thought processes, is not.

In 2001 Peavey came to Australia and ran a series of workshops, one of which was in western Sydney. I took myself up from Canberra for a one-day workshop on the first level – what is – and found it very worthwhile. I followed up a week later with a two-day workshop on the second level – what could be. This was equally stimulating and worthwhile. On the second day, Peavey paired the participants up and sent us off into the main street of suburban Richmond to put our strategic questioning skills to use. Our task was to strike up a conversation with a stranger, explain the training we were doing, and enquire how they were feeling about Aboriginal Reconciliation.

This was five years into John Howard's reign during which symbolism and any notion of Aboriginal rights was under attack or ditched in favour of practical reconciliation. Health, education, housing and employment became the focus. These replaced educating the wider community, a commitment to address underlying disadvantage and investigating some form of document of reconciliation.

Howard had adopted the view of historian Geoffrey Blainey that much of the historical account of European settlement, or invasion, of Australia had been overly negative. In 1993 Blainey termed this a 'black armband view of history,' being too focused on imperialism, exploitation and racism. Not to mention massacres. Another historian, Henry Reynolds, responded a black armband was preferable to a white blindfold. Indigenous issues were never far from the headlines. Controversy and polarisation was the norm in the regular skirmishes that underlined the culture wars. Sadly, that continues to this day.

I was paired with a young woman of Asian background. She was, I reckon, about 150cm tall (which is about 35 cm shorter than me) and 50kgs ringing wet (which is about 50kg lighter than me). We made a notable pair. Our victim was a fellow who had just put the shopping into his car, now leaning against it lighting a cigarette. We approached, explained our purpose and enquired on how he was feeling about Aboriginal Reconciliation.

Turns out he wasn't feeling so good about it. Quite badly in fact. We used the strategic questioning process which helped him establish what he knew, and, importantly, how he knew it. After initially venting his frustration at what he saw as unfair advantages available only to Aboriginal people, he volunteered that his knowledge came from talk back radio. And he didn't know any Aboriginal people. He could see there were big gaps in his knowledge and he wasn't certain of its accuracy. Towards the end of our conversation, which went through two cigarettes, he expressed the view that there had to be a better way of managing Aboriginal affairs. Quite a change, after weathering the initial storm. My partner and I were convinced of the value of the strategic questioning process. And I was hooked.

Another process in Meg's yellow folder was a questioning technique known as the Focused Conversation Method. This used four levels of questioning: Objective, Reflective, Interpretational and Decisional. The process is sometimes known by the acronym ORID.

Objective questions set the scene and establish the facts. Reflective questions establish individual feelings and responses to the issue or question. Interpretive questions establish greater understanding and identify the importance of the issue. Decisional questions draw conclusions and identify future actions. I found this too, to be immensely useful.

Almost subconsciously I have blended the two methods, Strategic Questioning and Focused Conversation Method, and have used them with groups of all sizes and in my own individual thought processes.

As a 'satisfactory' horticulturist, and a thinking one, I know that a slow growing tree is likely to be stronger and longer-lived than a fast growing tree. And so it is with decision making.

As French essayist Joseph Joubert said: 'It is better to debate a question without settling it, than to settle a question without debating it.' While there is a tendency for individuals or groups to feel the need to rush to a quick decision and get on with it, a well-considered decision that considers all aspects of a question or issue is likely to be a better decision. More durable, longer lasting. Like a slow growing tree.

For a while I offered a workshop for community service workers: Focussed and Strategic Questioning used the two methods. This was essentially a workshop in slow decision making. Not widely in demand, you could say this was a niche market. I told you I was unemployable.

A year or so after the Peavey workshops I found myself with a full-time position in Sydney. (More on that later.) Here, I had the chance to participate in a program at the Mt Eliza Business School, near Melbourne. Thinking Strategically was a three-day live-in program at what is widely seen as an elite institution. Someone else had booked a place on this but something came up and he was unable to take it on. As a refund wasn't possible it was offered to me.

Group think is a phenomenon that arises when the wish for full agreement or harmony overrides a dysfunctional decision making process, refusing to engage with alternatives, disallowing scepticism. The bombing of Pearl Harbor in the second world war is an often quoted example. Senior officers at Pearl Harbor ignored warnings from Washington DC about potential invasion because they didn't believe Japan would start a war with the United States.

And here at Mt Eliza, I found group think well on display.

I took my place among 16 participants from major industries such as mining, transport, telecommunications, gaming and a smattering of government agencies. Two participants were women. As an education and training manager at a national youth development program, I stood out somewhat.

The program was conducted under Chatham House Rule, Chatham House being the home of the Royal Institute of International Affairs in London. The rule, now used around the world, aims to encourage open discussion and sharing of information on sensitive issues. Speakers can share their individual views in private, but they remain private and confidential, with only the broader debate being made public. You may question my commitment to the rules.

It was a full program with plenary sessions, small group work and case studies of successful industries or businesses. The Australian wine industry was one case study, with much of its growth being attributed to marketing, particularly Alcopops targeting young women. Alcopops are sweetly flavoured drinks, so sweet that many mask the taste of alcohol. Often of lower alcohol content they are seen by some as a bridge for those not yet well accustomed to the taste of alcohol.

Having seen the impact of these on young women and girls I voiced a view that the industry had some responsibility for the harm this can cause, the social impact. None of those in my cohort shared my view, or if they did, they weren't able to express it. The group norm can smother dissent.

A paper from the Harvard Business School was the basis of another case study, this time lauding the transformation over two decades of General Electric, under a dynamic and visionary leader. The paper opened with: 'Jack Welch glowed with pride at General Electric's Annual Meeting in March 1999.' Revenues were up, margins at all-time highs, earnings per share increased. All marvellous stuff. The paper went on to detail Welch's management approach, getting rid of red tape, irrelevancies and staff. All staff were reviewed annually and the bottom 10 per cent were sacked. No if's, but's or how come's. Just sacked.

I accept the reality that some people are incompetent or just unsuited to the position they are in. There will always be a need to dismiss some people. But I've read the *Peter Principle* which spells out how people in a hierarchy, based on their success in one position, are promoted to another level at which they are incompetent and cannot possibly succeed. I have seen management incompetence and refusal to acknowledge errors of judgement interwoven with unethical behaviour. And I think a hard and fast rule that the bottom 10 per cent be sacked is abysmal.

Once again there was no comment on my view, and it didn't warrant a response from either the course leader or any other participants. As I see it, a more holistic approach to learning would be to explore different views, which is not to say endorse them. Understanding views you don't agree with is an important life skill.

Feeling as a fish out of water may, I went for broke, wondering out loud if John Howard's wish for Australia to be the world's greatest shareholding democracy is what we really want to be. I may as well have farted.

One of life's rich learning experiences was my three days at the Mt Eliza Business School, but my sceptical self was pleased to leave.

Playing make believe

Let me introduce you to a young boy known as Peanut. James Delarue is his real name but, with affection, everyone calls him Peanut. Peanut lives with his parents and older sister in the rough and ready country town of Boomeroo. Eight blocks long and four blocks wide, that's Boomeroo. This is a small town where everyone knows everyone's business, and if they don't, they'd be likely to make it up.

Peanut has a best friend and constant companion by the name of Jack Rivers. If Peanut has a game going on, one of life's mysteries to be explored, or just a stretch of daydreaming to be done, then Jack will be in it. Peanut's family have mixed reactions to Jack.

Nance, Peanut's mother, is very fond – perhaps too fond – of Jack. She includes him in all the family's activities and there's always a place at the kitchen table. Father Tony tolerates but doesn't understand his son's relationship with Jack. As for Peanut's sister Connie, well, she's a big sister and a bossy one.

Peanut and Jack star in *Jack Rivers and Me*, a novel set in the 1950s. In 1980 the book was awarded The Australian/ Vogel Literary Award for writers under age 35. The following year it was published and its author, Paul Radley, was named Young Australian of the Year. In the mid 1990s the book again captured attention.

I read *Jack Rivers* at a time of life where some equanimity was on the horizon, after a lengthy period of turbulence. This was my first book of literary fiction since high school. I doubt I could have read it during the turbulent days. Wouldn't have had the focus. The central theme of *Jack Rivers* is the power of imagination and the hold this can take on people. It has lessons for some of life's mysteries. Religion, in particular.

I grew up with only a modicum of religion in my life. Sunday School didn't appeal and didn't last long and there was no parental coercion to stick at it. I got an exclusion from religious instruction at high school without any fuss. Basically, religion – I'd like to say any religion, but I really only knew Christianity – just didn't make sense. Too much make-believe. Big-man-in-the-sky? Virgin birth? I mean, really. I was a sceptic before I knew what a sceptic was.

Religion tells people what is true or false, right or wrong. It commands people to have faith, to believe without question. Religion resolutely denies observation and evidence to support that faith. I'm no scientist but I understand the scientific process, which seeks to form a view on observation and evidence. Science continually questions its own observation and evidence and the views it forms.

To put it starkly, science asks questions that may never be answered, while religion provides answers that must never be questioned. Talk about chalk and cheese.

Questioning what I believe, and why, has long been important to me. Somewhere around the time I read *Jack Rivers* (close to 40 years ago), I tried to form a more considered view on religion. Why was it I didn't believe? Shouldn't there be more to a well-considered view than 'it just didn't make sense.' I pondered this for some time and then, in the way that first thoughts sometimes prove most durable, concluded 'it just didn't make sense.' And, although I still occasionally think on it, that's been good enough for me ever since.

By thinking things through, questioning own beliefs, particularly the deep-seated beliefs, we address what Hannah Arendt called the life of the mind. This distinguishes truth and meaning, knowing and thinking. Thinking links our active life and our contemplative mind. This is what reflective memoir writing or a persuasive personal essay does. Writing that goes beyond recording mere facts, but aims to understand, make sense and see connections between the personal and the universal. Writing helps think things through. It's slower and it's different to just thinking things through. Or, as novelist and essayist E.M. Forster has said: 'How do I know what I think until I see what I say.'

My atheism, or more correctly pan-atheism, doesn't preclude a sense of spirituality, which I grappled with for years. I now understand spirituality to be an acceptance there is more to the world than the material. The pinnacle is the inner life of self-knowledge which captures the emotional realm and offers empathy and compassion to all things in their beauty, awe and wonder. From a swirl of gas and dust our world evolved several billion years ago to give us mountain ranges and desert plains, oceans, lakes and rivers, forest giants and weedy nuisances, blue whales and bush ticks. How not to be in awe, feel a sense of reverence?

Believers in a god claim many virtues but claiming religion as the basis of morality is laden with hubris. The golden rule applies to any form of behaviour, any code of conduct, not just that claimed by religion. For the great majority of us knowing right from wrong isn't that hard. Everyone has the capacity for good and evil, but I believe people to be good by nature unless damaged through addiction, abuse or pernicious role models.

Religion supposedly encourages people to be nice to each other. To be compassionate, cooperative, charitable. Its rituals appeal to a sense of the aesthetic and it supports a sense of community and social cohesion. All of this can support a calm mind. Undoubtedly these are personal and societal goods, but they are freely available in the Op Shop, the Landcare group, the service club. Anywhere people meet.

The 2021 Australian Census showed in the previous 10 years the number of people reporting no religion had increased from 22% to 39%. Over the same period the number of people who identify as Christian had fallen from 61% to 44%. Hinduism and Islam are growing but make up a very small percentage of the population.

The figures for those reporting a religious belief are likely overstated as people routinely identify a religion they were born into, rather than a current religious conviction or adherence. Parents also assign their religious beliefs to their children.

A 2017 Ipsos Global Poll revealed almost two thirds of Australians think religion does more harm than good. Yet throughout Australia, parliaments and local councils – where we find people who claim to be providing leadership – start their meetings with a prayer to the almighty. You would have to wonder why this continues, how long it can continue.

So back to *Jack Rivers*. Despite his constant and very real presence throughout the Delarue family, he doesn't actually exist. He's Peanut's imaginary friend.

As the time approaches for Peanut to start school Connie worries that Peanut, with an imaginary friend, will not survive the mockery that will surely come his way. She campaigns for Jack to be sent away. Peanut resists, with help from Nance. But Connie persists, and finally prevails.

Cutting it fine you might say, but on the morning of his first day at school, Peanut announces that Jack has gone to the outback for a while, droving. After that he'll be going to the islands. Peanut has a good imagination – that's the basis of Jack's place in the scheme of things – but Peanut has accepted reality, realising he doesn't need Jack any more. Just an ordinary part of growing up. Everyone does it and, along with the power of imagination, this is the essence of *Jack Rivers and Me*.

After Jack Rivers left Boomeroo the sky didn't fall in. Peanut got on with his life and grew to be a fine person. Father Tony had never been close to Peanut and had been almost resentful of his son's relationship with Jack. But when Jack left the father-son relationship blossomed. For mother Nance, Jack was a permutation of a former boyfriend who had died in the war. Jack's leaving helped her move on.

In 1996 Paul Radley revealed, on national television, that it was his uncle and not he who had written *Jack Rivers and Me*. Radley said his life had been ruined by the duplicity and the torment he felt. I hope he recovered well; we all make mistakes.

Falsehoods, like false beliefs though, are not good for anyone. In the mid 19th century Karl Marx said religion: '… is the opium of the people,' disconnecting the disadvantaged from their situation, offering relief from reality as a means of political control. As the Roman philosopher Lucius Annaeus Seneca had put it back in the first century: 'Religion is regarded by the common people as true, by the wise as false, and by the rulers as useful.'

On the other hand, facing reality, questioning personal beliefs along with societal dogmas, and perhaps waving goodbye to imaginary friends – just as Peanut did – can be positively enriching. Whether religion, political leanings or acceptance of any of the institutions of modern life, you may like to think about it.

On the personal essay

If the aim of the personal essay is to convince a reader of the argument you are making, or at least nudge them in that direction, you might consider the three components of persuasive rhetoric as proposed by the Greek philosopher Aristotle, who lived 384-322 BC.

The first of these is ethos or credibility. Does the writer know what she or he is talking about? Is there a recognisable element of authority, of respect? How has that knowledge been acquired? Is it up to date?

The second is pathos, or the emotional appeal to the reader. Vivid language and sensory detail can help readers relate to the writer's personal experience. This may also connect with the reader's experience.

The third is logos, or the logic and reasoning used. Is the argument and the evidence consistent and reliable throughout or are there gaps and questionable assertions which throw doubt on the whole argument?

You may, to a greater or lesser extent, have seen these components in the previous personal essay.

Hard roads

After a couple of years Meg found the bastardry of the public service under a cost-cutting Liberal government difficult to deal with. During times of distress she was enduring, we discussed her options and decided there was only one that was realistic in the short term. Real Options became the name of the business we established when she left the ACT Parks Service for the greener pastures of self-employment with me. Not being wedded to the goal of a superannuation nest egg some years ahead made the decision easier.

Our initial focus was on the development of community education programs in the environmental, health and community sectors. We had some immediate success although the work that we were able to compete for changed over the years. There was endless adaptation and re-invention, a great deal of fun and much uncertainty.

We were essentially offering communitarianism in a capitalist system. This is about connections between individuals and their community relationships with a reduced focus on individualism. Nothing to do with communism or socialism, but still, more niche work. I've always been attracted to hard roads. It's why we were able to work in the community services sector, but struggled to find a way into vocational training where the private providers are focused on corporate success.

One of our major projects was the development of a community education program on civics and citizenship. Civics is about understanding how government and society operate, while citizenship is about playing an active part. I can't say with any certainty that our work on the civics and citizenship front educated many Australians, but I can say with absolute certainty that I learnt a lot. And this has influenced very much of what I have done professionally and publicly ever since.

The program used an informal adult learning method known as a study circle, a small group of people who meet informally a number of times to learn about an issue of importance or interest to them. It relies on facilitation, usually by a group member, and concise information, sometimes using the bi-line: 'without a teacher or a textbook.' The study circle presents a range of discussion questions to help people deal with complex issues and competing viewpoints. The ideal conditions for a study circle are not always easy to put in place, but when it works well it is as good as adult education gets. The method has been part of the fabric of Swedish society since the early 20th century. But Australia is not Sweden. Apart from the civics and citizenship program, we had other work using the study circle method on environmental issues and health promotion.

The civics and citizenship program was also spectacular for the size of our contract. With two study circles to develop, a rigorous and extensive development approach, one thousand copies of each to be printed and national distribution the total contract value was $230,000. Way beyond anything else. A couple of days before the end of the financial year, just after we had signed the contract, the department rang. They were trying to clear their books and wondered if we would mind if they paid us $170,000 up front. We didn't mind. But didn't bank the cheque until July 1. At this time the accountant advised we should incorporate the business as a company. That way if anything should go bad financially, we get to keep the house. Real Options became Real Options Pty Ltd.

During our work on this program, a colleague with far greater experience in adult education, Bob Boughton, summed up the major challenge;

> The problem is not that people don't know the difference between the House of Representatives and the Senate [in

Canberra], the problem is people know they don't know the difference, but they don't think it matters.

A Parliament of Australia research paper on active citizenship, from 1999, but arguably more relevant than ever, tells us;

> Our system of government relies for its efficacy and legitimacy on an informed citizenry; without active, knowledgeable citizens the forms of democratic representation remain empty; without vigilant, informed citizens there is no check on potential tyranny.

These statements, that people don't think their ignorance matters, and that it really does, have stayed with me and influence much of what I do to this day.

During our flurry of study circle activity we had a couple of programs to develop for the Murray Darling Basin Commission, the predecessor to the Murray Darling Basin Authority. The Commission's then Director of Education and Communications, David Eastburn, who became and remains a friend, had engaged the Australian Association of Adult and Community Education (AAACE), who then contracted us. Eastburn had a broad view of the Commission's role, which included testing new approaches and study circles was new to the natural resource management and agriculture sectors.

Soon after starting on our first study circle project, on Dryland Salinity, we realised a need to help people understand the process of the study circle, which is different to traditional educational approaches as it is very much learner centred and self-directed. On contentious issues it provides a range of viewpoints for participants to consider as they form their own view. This is uncommon practice. Most educational programs will present the sponsors view, whether the sponsor be a government agency, an industry or community organisation. In that sense it is propaganda.

We settled on the idea of an informal discussion guide. This is a mini version of a study circle intended for use in a single session, to give an experience of a study circle and build confidence in the approach. In wanting to focus on the process, rather than the content we decided an entirely unrelated subject would be best. So Plastic Shopping Bags it was. If the guide had been on dryland salinity, people would incline to a focus on the subject matter.

Facts and figures were obtained and included in relation to numbers of bags used, numbers recycled and both positive and negative environmental effects. Yes, there are positives. It presented a number of approaches to managing problems: education, regulation or imposition of penalties for littering.

Viewpoints from the Commonwealth Environment Department, Clean Up Australia, the Australian Conservation Foundation and the Plastics and Chemicals Industry Association (PACIA) were also included. This information was readily available from all, except PACIA.

In my first phone call to PACIA I explained the project and that no particular stance is taken, just facts, viewpoints and a process to help with decision making. I followed up seeking the response that was promised but didn't come. At one stage they advised they were not cooperating because I could well be: 'an aggressive, anti-plastic shopping bag activist.' I may have been, but there was nothing in my communication with them to support that position.

Ultimately I was able to cajole enough words out of them to make the discussion guide complete. Realisation that the words, 'Declined to comment,' below their name would not be a good look may have altered their stance.

A little later on Meg and I, along with a couple of colleagues, hatched the idea of developing monthly informal discussion guides following the same approach on major issues facing Australia. These included school funding, gambling, bullying, mutual obligation, sustainability and leadership. We called this *More Than Just Talk*. Each of these guides took a great deal of time and we learnt a great deal over a year before succumbing to the incompetence of our marketing. We ran out of steam. The illustrator we employed made more than we did.

Around this time, a group of unemployed young people I was working with in Canberra developed a guide on the issue of managing the over population of kangaroos in an ACT Nature Reserve. This was based on culling by professional shooters and was quite a contentious issue at the time, with a range of strongly held viewpoints. The discussion guide was well received until a senior public servant in the ACT Parks Service objected to airing the animal liberation view. This was completely opposite to the Parks Service practice, and not to be given any space. Controlling the public debate is important to bureaucracies.

For about seven years until 2012 Real Options held a contract with Shoalhaven City Council to deliver support to voluntary Bushcare groups who worked on council controlled reserves. As in many areas, conflict arose when nearby residents believed they had a right to a water view, and that right should not be impeded by trees, whether they were original or replanted. Shoalhaven was a national leader in vandalism of trees on public reserves.

While there is no proprietary right to a view in law, many of the dominant group of councillors supported the residents' view. The issue was highly politicised at the local level where councillors devoted a great deal of time to oversight of the Bushcare program. This extended to prescribing the maximum height of any plantings.

The period of our contract included the time when I held a public role in a major campaign against the dominant group of Shoalhaven councillors. When the campaign was at its most intense, the contract kept us afloat at a subsistence level. While Meg and I were aware we might lose the contract due to my public activities, this was a possibility we were prepared for.

Within local government the awarding of a contract is an operational matter to be determined by staff. Beyond setting policy, elected councillors should have no role in this. At least that's the theory. I suspect the reason we kept the contract is simply that the councillors did not know of its existence. This came unstuck when I agreed to facilitate a public meeting about a bushland reserve. At this meeting was a local councillor.

Shortly after that public meeting, at a council general meeting, a couple of councillors asked questions of the general manager about the circumstances of my engagement by council. One, in particular, used the phrase: 'given his political activities.'

When I asked the councillor to explain the reason for his request, he refused, beyond saying he can ask any questions he likes that are in the public interest or to better inform himself. I believe the purpose was to discriminate against me. The consequences of his action would be a clear message to staff not to engage me or our business in future.

I reported this to council's general manager, asking that the matter be referred to council's conduct committee. He refused, stating that decisions on engaging services such as those we provided was an operational matter, decided by staff.

It was the case that council staff were reviewing the contract at that time, looking at all possible means to support Bushcare groups. A few months later, following that review, our contract was not renewed. This may well have been the outcome without any political interference. As I said, councillors do not interfere in operational matters. In theory. But it is not difficult to see how his action could be construed as influencing the decision.

The first study circle for the Murray Darling Basin Commission on Dryland Salinity by necessity had a narrow focus and a limited audience. It's fair to say it didn't set the world on fire, and indeed there were some in the natural resource management community who saw their role as opposing anything that wasn't their idea. A widespread human trait. However, its availability created an understanding of the approach and, arguably, laid the ground for the next of the study circles, on Sustainable

Rivers. As every human activity on land has some impact on a river, this had a much broader focus and, potentially unlimited audience.

The subject demanded a holistic worldview and the approach we took was that there were no environmental problems per se, just a whole bunch of social, economic and political problems that affect the environment. We also posited that science, engineering and technology had much to offer in achieving a level of sustainability, but didn't have all the answers. Things were bad with our rivers and change was needed. (And this was 1999!) The change needed to strengthen community resilience and capacity to respond.

As is the way of bureaucracies a steering committee was established and met at the commencement of our work. While working on the program for close to a year we provided updates and drafts to the steering committee with a comforting level of support from all except chairman Rob, a water engineer at the Commission. We heard virtually nothing from him until a second steering committee meeting convened to review a complete draft of the program.

Members of the steering committee chatted amiably, catching up on the latest news over a coffee before the meeting started. Kind thoughts were offered on the comprehensive and engaging nature of the draft we had worked long and hard on, and felt well pleased by. But this state of self-satisfaction was about to crack.

Chairman Rob opened the meeting by saying he wanted to welcome everyone in attendance, but first he needed to note how completely unsatisfactory the draft's content was, being loaded with false information and having an anti-science bias. What followed is best described as a five-hour shit fight broken only by a frosty lunch.

The then director of the Australian Association for Adult and Community Education was part of the steering committee and took up the challenge of defending the study circle approach, which chairman Rob didn't understand. The others in the committee were mostly of a technical background. Despite their support for the content during the development period, and just prior to the meeting starting, they were unable or unwilling to defend our work against chairman Rob. Eye contact was avoided and much uneasy shifting of bums in seats took place as a belligerent tirade was unleashed.

Not a single acknowledgement was made of any useful content in the work we had produced. Chairman Rob later had Susan, a young understudy, go through the draft and note areas of dispute. There was barely a paragraph left unmarked by her red pen, let alone a page. She has gone on to a wonderful career.

If chairman Rob was high priest of the Cult of Scientific Certainty, Meg and I were devil worshippers from the Cult of Eco-doom. The upshot was the Commission sacked the director of the Communications Department who had engaged Real Options and undertook a review of the Dryland Salinity program. Unsurprisingly the review provided the justification needed to cancel the Sustainable Rivers program. Once again, the required level of control over a message had proven compelling.

In retrospect – my sage in the sky, again – we might have foreseen problems with chairman Rob's hands-off approach until the end, and taken steps to try and prevent the outcome. Retrospect is always wise, but because I won't be beaten by ignorance or bullying this was one of life's rich learning experiences. 'What does not kill me,' German philosopher Frederick Nietzsche said, 'makes me stronger.' At this time Meg and I had thick enough skins to survive this bruising encounter, though I can't help but wonder how someone younger and less experienced would have coped.

Corrupting the youth

Another key lesson on the level of control governments demand, and the extent to which public servants and hired help will go to satisfy their political masters, came in 2001. Meg and I were hired as casual facilitators to work with participants in a Commonwealth Government Youth Roundtable. This was the third annual roundtable in which a group of about 50 young people from around Australia were chosen and supported throughout the year to plan, develop and implement a project of importance to them and their community. Participants would meet twice during the year.

The roundtable was announced in 1998 at the same time the Commonwealth Government defunded the Australian Youth Policy and Action Coalition (AYPAC) which had been established in the late 1970s as the national peak body for youth affairs.

A few years after the demise of AYPAC, a new body, the Australian Youth Affairs Coalition (AYAC), was established. From 2002-2008 it operated without government funding. When the Labor Government was elected in 2008 it provided funding to AYAC. In 2014 when Labor was defeated and the Coalition Government was elected, AYAC was defunded. The pattern was clear, although with good reason members of AYAC expressed little confidence in either of the major parties ability to work well with youth.

But back to 2001, when we were required to attend Youth Roundtable facilitator training in Melbourne, presented by the government department with oversight of the roundtable, the Department of Education, Training and Youth Affairs (DETYA), and their hired help, the YMCA.

During the first of a two-day training program our group of facilitators-in-training were told of problems that had arisen during previous years' roundtables, including that some participants had wanted to meet with an opposition party spokesperson. I was surprised this was seen as a problem, and expressed a view that people make their best decisions when they receive information from a range of sources. 'Be very clear,' our group was told by the department's project manager, 'this is the government's Youth Roundtable. Not the opposition's or the Democrats.'

Other problems, we were told, arose from participant's inexperience with the media. In a clear reference to the Howard government's refusal to offer an apology to the Stolen Generation, one had worn a SORRY T-shirt during their project presentation, with the media present. Inexperience, or media savvy, I wonder?

Another had given an interview to Triple J early in the roundtable process when he was unhappy about a number of things. Triple J played the interview on the day of his presentation when he had worked through the issues and regretted the interview. Or so we were told.

At the start of the second day's training I was taken aside by the YMCA representative and told of concerns about my professionalism, and that I appeared to lack confidence. My views about seeking a wide range of information sources were also badly received. To top it off, someone from the DETYA team, a Mr McDonald or MacDonald, had been offended I got their name wrong. Sometimes there's a perceived need to intensify or overstate a problem, to make matters seem worse than they really are. We can all do this. But that was pretty desperate.

The day after the training, before leaving for home, we had a visit from the YMCA hired hand delivering the news our services were not required. My first impulse was to make a public statement about what I viewed as political interference and control over a youth consultation program. A colleague, with much greater experience of working with government, cautioned against this. 'If you make a public statement about this,' he said, 'you will never get another government contract, no matter what side of politics is in government.' I stewed over this but followed the advice. And felt self-loathing for years as a result.

There was more annoyance when the YMCA refused to pay what we were owed, including travel costs to Melbourne, until we had a solicitor send a letter pointing out we had done all that was required of us and legal action would follow if they didn't pay. They coughed up immediately. Once again an astounding level of control from a bureaucracy. All in all, another of life's rich learning experiences, you could say.

In May 2014 when announcing it was stripping funding from AYAC, Parliamentary Secretary to the Minister for Education, Scott Ryan, said;

> This government does not believe that a single peak body is necessary for it to hear the views of Australian youth, nor that a single peak body is capable of representing the diverse interests, experiences and background of young Australians.

He added;

> The government is currently developing plans to consult with young Australians using a more focused and targeted approach.

I sought information from the minister's office but none was available. I followed up six months later. Still no information was available. A personable staffer in the minister's office told me, quite cheerily, but off the record, none would be forthcoming. There were no such plans, nothing was done or would be done.

I wrote about this for *New Matilda*, an on-line news site, referencing qualitative research from several years earlier into the experience of a select number of participants over the first six years of the Roundtable. This found the Roundtable to be politically manipulated and that participants shifted: 'From being engaged, excited and hopeful to being hurt, disillusioned and disenchanted,' with feelings of exclusion from the political process. Of more than 200 recommendations made during the six years of the study, just six were accepted. The report raised crucial and fundamental questions about how governments engage with youth, suggesting a radical re-think was required. That Labor did badly when in government was also noted.

Clearly, a well-established independent national peak body is more representative than a one-off program for individuals. The national body develops experience, memory and capacity, becoming increasingly effective. Perhaps increasingly annoying. And governments, particularly the Coalition variety, have long lacked a soft spot for those peak bodies prone to offering unwelcome advice.

The ancient Greek philosopher Socrates was known for questioning the notion that might makes right. In 399BC he was sentenced to death for challenging the accepted gods and corrupting the minds of the youth. In my view the Australian government approach to political engagement with youth has a corrupting affect. I finished my piece to *New Matilda* by repeating the Parliamentary Secretary's claim, with my own take on their duplicity, italicised below;

The government is currently developing plans,
>*this may take some time,*

to consult with young Australians,
>*ticking boxes really, we've already decided,*

using a more focused and targeted approach
>*to ignore those with a broad view, a national perspective.*
>>*To be honest you see,*
>>>*we find this rather bothersome.*

A small balm to the sense of disappointment in myself I had carried for many years.

The Ideas Factory

The setting: our kitchen/ dining room at Huskisson, one Saturday morning.

>Meg: [out of the blue while idly flicking through the paper] There's a job here in Sydney you should go for.
>
>Me: [at my flippant best] Don't be silly. Who wants a job, and in Sydney?

But Meg was right. The business was struggling, I was discontented teaching at TAFE and we hadn't well settled into life at Jervis Bay. I was in my late 40s and future job opportunities of the sort that were up my alley would be limited. Sydney would be an interesting challenge and the Huskisson house would still be there.

Fast forward several weeks and I walked out of an interview feeling supremely confident. National Training Manager for the Green Corps youth development program brought together my interests in working with unemployed young people and the environment. Right up my alley.

Green Corps had been operating for several years, administered by an environmental volunteer organisation. This was at the start of new contract arrangements and was a partnership between Job Futures, an employment services provider, and Greening Australia, the environmental organisation I had worked for ten years earlier. One organisation's focus was on environmental outcomes, the other's on personal development and employment outcomes. It seemed a natural fit, a highly complementary partnership.

My interviewees, the two chief executives, accepted everything I had to say, including a proposal that the position be called National *Education* and Training Manager. If I was in the position the focus would be on life-long and self-directed learning, and not just vocational training.

This was a three-year contract but we made the decision to take it one year at a time. I was surprisingly nervous starting the job. Not only a loss of independence but worried my values may not align. Like most people I had had experiences of workplace disharmony before, and made myself unpopular getting involved in management decisions that had no direct impact on me but affected others unfairly. Part of my unemployability.

I have a problem with heights so on my first day in the 18th floor office I asked not to be near a window. I wound up in a store room which I named the Bat Cave. Seven people worked in the national office: six located with Job Futures in Sydney, and one outpost in Canberra, at Greening Australia. These seven people would have to bond, develop and find a workable relationship with a broader group based at Greening Australia offices in all the capital cities.

While planning our relocation, Meg and I made a conscious decision to move to the opposite of Jervis Bay, a fairly monocultural population with immense areas of open space. So we targeted Marrickville in Sydney's inner west, with very high diversity in its resident population and a miniscule area of open space. It was only on moving in we realised we were directly under the Sydney airport flight path. The windows fairly rattled, the light shades danced, ready to unleash their immense aggravational potential. Somehow or other they knew when I had a bad day in the office, and there were more than a few of those.

On starting I quickly bonded to the notion of Green Corps operating as an ideas factory, being open to possibilities, taking off the straight jacket the previous program administrators had applied, making a real difference to the lives of the young people. These notions were part of the vernacular. As was a commitment to workplace democracy, where people had a right to be involved in decisions that affected them.

Big ideas need resources and money was short. Change was needed. In retrospect the process was hazy, details vague, questions unanswered. Sacrificing the national office outpost position in Canberra was mooted as a possibility. But the person in that position was not engaged in this discussion. Talking the talk on workplace democracy didn't lead to walking the walk.

Nick was not a great mate of mine, but he was a decent fellow doing his job as best he could. It's arguable that this position was badly conceived in the first place. And it's fair to say that management has to manage, has to make decisions, including hard ones. But following a proper process is part of this and what was happening here was far more than a failure of the position or the incumbent, but a failure of management. I couldn't cop this so I called Nick and told him what was likely coming his way. And then sat back and waited to be asked if I knew how he came across the news. But the question never came.

This was the starkest example of the management approach to decision making that I encountered, and felt dismayed by. That experience was not dissimilar to a far more direct conflict I had 10 years earlier, also with management dealings with staff. While not having a direct impact on me, these were situations I could not live with.

My experience of self-employment from a young age had provided independence and control which more than compensated for financial uncertainty. Combined with a strong sense of justice and revulsion for needless interference I did not make a good employee.

Some months on I resigned, lasting just one year into the three-year contract. I had some great moments, a few shockers, and like to think I made a useful contribution. But no more Bat Cave.

March fly lessons

Anyone who has ever been bitten by a March fly knows how painful this can be. These large dark flies are found throughout Australia, most commonly during summer, not March. It's the females which suck blood, bringing them to our attention, while the more pleasantly benign males suck nectar. Wave a female March fly away and it will likely return. Persistence is a characteristic.

They have one inherent weakness in that they often land and take a few seconds, perhaps concentrating on their task, before biting. This allows time for a defensive slap, but they are amazingly resilient. Slap one down and, unless it's a fatal blow, watch it lay motionless on the ground. Watch a little longer and a slow revival often comes. First a small shudder of the wings. Then it may get itself right way up. Another shrug or two and then it's back on the wing, seemingly fully recovered. Quite remarkable.

In the late 1990s while living in Canberra I had an agreement with a fellow I had met socially to research and contribute written content for a book on natural resource management. This was to be produced for a government department who had contracted the other fellow. I had expertise in specific areas I was to be responsible for and formed half of his project team. Looking at the proposal one sensed that we met the requirements and were a good match. We weren't.

I was to be paid $7,000 and received $4,500 up front. It quite quickly became apparent our different approaches to the job were incompatible. In a nutshell he thought I wasn't completing the work quickly enough, I felt he was trying to micro-manage me, constantly changing dates when tasks were to be completed. Whatever friendship we had quickly dissolved and within a couple of months my former friend (MFF) sacked me and asked for the advance I had received to be repaid. I thought my sacking was unreasonable and refused.

Shortly after that I received a solicitor's letter demanding payment. I did what you do and found a solicitor to reply, stating that as I had been terminated, I had been denied the opportunity to complete the work and be paid the remaining amount. My solicitor also suggested MFF and I attend conflict resolution. A second letter came, ignoring the suggested conflict resolution while re-stating the original demand. My solicitor thought it huffing and puffing and suggested ignoring it, which I did, before proceeding to forget all about it.

Fast forward several years and, as if channelling a March fly, MFF resurfaced. Just one week before the six-year limitation period expired he started proceedings in the ACT Small Claims Court. This sought the $4,500 I had been paid plus interest, now nearly $7,000 all up by his calculations.

The court registrar arranged a pre-hearing conference to see if a resolution or compromise could be reached before going to court. The minimum amount MFF would accept was $4,500, magnanimously agreeing to forgo the interest if I agreed to pay that amount. I don't need to occupy the high moral ground but prefer it to the alternative. I declined the offer.

The Small Claims Court is intended for people to represent themselves. Although legal representation is allowed there is no opportunity for the successful party to claim costs. It's handy having a solicitor in the family and MFF made good use of his. I was tempted to represent myself because it seemed the right thing to do, in keeping with the spirit of the court, but in the end I hired a solicitor, just starting his own practice and available at better than market rates.

I prepared for the court hearing as best I could, hampered by incomplete memory of events more than six years earlier and the lack of records and any work associated with this project. When we had moved to the south coast I had recycled a mass of paperwork including all records of this ill-fated job. Legally this material should have been kept for six years. The fact I didn't know this didn't matter.

The hearing went over two days and started with the magistrate enquiring about attempts to resolve the dispute. It's very rare, she said, for either party to be entirely satisfied with the result. MFF had one witness, I had three, all of whom had some role in the contract at the department.

With no documentary evidence my case was weaker than it may have been. My witnesses' evidence that having me as part of the project team was a major factor in MFF winning the contract may have been helpful to my case. That MFF had his contract cancelled by the department after my sacking might also have helped. And that following the contract cancellation MFF had taken unsuccessful legal action against the department may have provided even more help.

While waiting for the decision I pondered the deliberative path the magistrate might follow. My solicitor thought there was no likelihood of the claim for interest being successful. Leaving proceedings to the last gasp of the six-year period without good reason went against this.

So, MFF wanted me to pay him $4,500. I wanted to pay him nothing. I reasoned that an experienced adjudicator, the magistrate in this case, would start at the mid-point which would be for me to pay $2,250. This amount would then be adjusted up in MFFs favour, or down in my favour, depending on the weight of the evidence.

In the end the magistrate awarded MFF $2,500. I have to say that additional $250 hurt disproportionately. My case, held over two days, got a 42 page written judgement which makes a good read. A high profile murder case around that time, and held over 16 days, only warranted 32 pages.

This was another of life's rich experiences, but one I wouldn't care to repeat. It's not often you get to watch at close quarters how the law works, how it balances legal rights and fairness. I was happy with my solicitor but wonder how I may have fared without him.

I now work as a professional mediator. I regularly deal with conflicts similar to my experience. Some of the skills I have learnt in mediation would have been handy all those years ago. What's the best possible outcome you might get? What's the worst possible outcome? How important is the high moral ground? Retrospect again. My sage in the sky.

⸺

'This will only take ten minutes,' the late middle-aged man, snappily dressed for the club, with an impressively firm handshake said, smiling broadly as I introduced myself. 'Do you think the other party will agree?' I asked, as his smile vanished. Club man was there for mediation, to try and resolve a conflict with his neighbour, which is not an uncommon situation. I was the mediator

In life, conflict is inevitable, but how we choose to deal with the conflict is optional. This applies as much to international affairs as it does to neighbours feuding over a fence, a tree or late-night noisy parties. An arbitrator or judge might make a decision, a ruling for or against the parties to the conflict. This usually produces a clear winner and a clear loser. Someone gets loaded up with resentment.

Mediation is entirely different with a third party, a mediator, entering the conflict. The parties have a problem, the mediator has a process. Each party needs to understand the process and accept the mediator's role as an independent, neutral facilitator, not as a decision maker.

Many neighbourhood mediations can be done in two or three hours. Complex issues may take longer, perhaps requiring multiple sessions. After reluctantly accepting ten minutes was unlikely, club man settled in for the long haul. And got to the club in plenty of time for happy hour, if not the lunch special.

Mediation starts with each party taking time to explain how it is for them. What has bought them to this point? This identifies issues for exploration. A bit like developing an agenda, collaboratively. The party's roles in the conflict comes into focus, along with the roles of other people.

While agreement on all aspects of the conflict isn't crucial, hearing the other party's perspective is.

Privately the parties have the chance to reflect on what the best possible outcome for them would be. And what would the worst outcome look like. This sets the scene for the pointy end of the mediation. Negotiation. What might they be able to offer the other party? What do they need in return? What can they agree on, stick to and not later regret?

Underlying issues are important. Previous history between the parties, positions within an organisation, or longevity and standing in a community can all come into play. As does the way one neighbour might have looked at another neighbour's spouse after a few drinks.

Power imbalances need to be identified and managed. Capacity to understand, listen, respond and articulate a point are not always equal. A lifetime of disadvantage isn't conducive to doing your best listening, empathising with the other. For some, being listened to fully and completely is a novel experience.

Applications for an Apprehended Personal Violence Order (APVO) are sometimes referred to mediation by a magistrate to give the parties a chance to reach agreement before the magistrate rules. These are where one party seeks protection from another who they are not in a domestic or family relationship with. In 2021/22 almost 4,600 APVO orders were issued in New South Wales. For the same period more than 34,000 Apprehended Domestic Violence Orders (ADVO) were issued where the parties are, or have been, in a domestic or family relationship. Staggering numbers which are increasing over recent years.

Impartiality is key to mediation. Any sort of existing relationship between the mediator and one of the parties is almost certain to lead to mistrust. A perception of bias will undermine the process. Beware the workplace supervisor who wants to mediate between two disputing employees.

Financial disputes between tradies and dissatisfied customers are common. Sometimes you get a sense the tradie has just stuffed the job. Other times you sense the customer is looking for any excuse not to pay.

Poor basic communication is always part of this. How else to explain a builder who thinks his customer is claiming around $8,000, while the customer, who initiated the mediation, is seeking around $180,000?

I have had a separated couple in dispute over their finances, having previously bought a house jointly. Though separated they remained friends with benefits, having spent the previous night together; just spooning I was told. It was cold. After tears and recriminations throughout the mediation they reached agreement and went off to a late lunch together. Very civilised.

In cooler climates I have a theory, completely unproven, that there is more neighbourhood conflict in the warmer months, when people are outside enjoying themselves and more likely to annoy neighbours. In the cooler months they are more likely to be inside, less likely to cause annoyance. This has been the experience during periods of lockdown in the pandemic that started in 2020.

I have been called a mongrel bastard as I terminated a mediation lacking a skerrick of good will or intention to mediate from one of the parties. I've been hugged, by both parties to an unexpectedly amicable agreement. I've felt genuine concern for the physical health of people who have themselves so worked up I'm mentally rehearsing my CPR. I've been troubled by those hearing voices, imagining things. And I've been moved to tears by two neighbouring couples, formerly friends before it all fell apart. Their solution revolved around preventing their respective children from playing together. Adults who can't sort their problems out and feel the only way forward is to use the kids. Un-bloody-believable. Four siblings who get along just fine – most of the time – have no way of agreeing on care for an elderly parent or the future of the family property. In a positive sign they all arrive together and sit together, waiting amiably. But when the issues close to their heart come to the fore they fall apart. Mediation is a great success.

Mediation reaches agreement in around 85 per cent of cases. Unlike a judgement handed down, a negotiated agreement between conflicted parties has some likelihood of preserving a relationship. It's likely to be a different relationship but, aiming as it does for understanding the others position, it may even be an enhanced relationship.

There's a problem-solving approach where an agreement needs to be reached over the fence or the tree or the amount of payment the parties will accept. But even these relatively straight forward mediations can aim to be transformational in the way that people learn to approach a conflict. There's a world of difference, for example, between fronting a neighbour to unload your problem, then and there, or raising the issue and seeking a mutually convenient time to discuss it. Understanding that and having it as a strategy for the next conflict that comes along is transformational. Coming to understand how others may see us, how a particular behaviour may be seen as threatening by someone else, can be life changing.

'When you find you are digging yourself into a hole,' a very wise person once said to me, 'the first thing to do is stop digging.' Not everyone recognises this and there's an element of coaching in mediation. As a mediator I ask myself if the parties have gained any insights into the way they have behaved in the conflict and responded in the mediation. If I haven't tried to plant a seed of self-reflection, I haven't done my job. What have you learnt, what might you do differently next time you find yourself in conflict, are good questions to pose as mediation comes to a close.

Clearly, some people have the persistence of a March fly. Looking back, from the position of what I now know, I have wondered what I would do differently when confronted by MFF's claim, six years after his perceived injustice. I don't seek the high moral ground in that I don't need to feel superior to others, but I do need to feel fair and consistent in my decisions and actions.

The only thing I can think of is being pragmatic, by making an offer to settle at the half way mark of the amount sought, excluding interest. Had this been accepted it would have avoided days of preparation and stress along with solicitor's costs. My feeling is MFF would not have accepted, he had the advantage of free legal support, and a fondness for litigation, but it would have been a fair and proactive way of approaching the conflict. I would have felt better for having made the attempt.

And now I also know, should any future conflict arise, to keep records as long as required. A sort of March fly repellent.

Public life

Interesting events are most interesting in memoir when some change happens and there are several accounts of change in the following four sections. In all of these there is some significant change in my personal and professional capacity. The first has a large element of my observing profound change in others. The story of community activism in the third section is a 'King dies, queen dies,' moment, 'after which the kingdom collapsed.' Storytelling, in other words, with a plot that details the magnitude of the task.

The tone you adopt can be varied, just as when speaking. Sometimes we speak seriously, sometimes light-heartedly. Sometimes philosophically, sometimes whimsically. Formal, crude, vulgar even. Changing tone needs attention and may be difficult within the same passage. It's probably better to change tone in a new paragraph or section. Perhaps after a break or dinkus.

Aim for a mix of short and long sentences. Long sentences can be demanding of the reader, though there are times when this may be needed. Short sentences, including non or partial sentences, can seem unnatural, staccato-like, though that can be helpful;

> Like a sharp poke in the ribs a short sentence has emphasis potential. It demands attention. See? I've just done it.

A palette of short, long and non-sentences provides the best opportunities. Varying paragraph size will also be helpful. This is all about the language used.

1. It's a common enough phenomenon that when people are faced with an issue they feel they should know about, but don't, they often have difficulty in saying, 'I don't know,' or 'I need more information.' Back in the late 1980s an American social scientist carried out research into people's attitude towards a piece of legislation, The 1975 Public Affairs Act. A large proportion of people in a random survey expressed either support or opposition to the Act. But the Act did not exist. You could expect a very similar outcome in Australia.

Using that and other research Jim Fishkin went on to develop the Deliberative Poll. This is a form of consultation that combines an opinion poll with deliberative democracy. Deliberative democracy is more about enabling citizens to participate in joint problem solving than merely inviting them to have a say. Having a say, which is the focus of most consultation between governments and citizens, is often nothing more than an exercise in tokenism, cynicism and manipulation. The consultation takes place after the decision has been made, even if the public are unaware of this, and follows the DAD approach: the decision is made, it is announced and is then defended. Deliberation means careful consideration before decision, which is the antithesis of many people's experiences of making choices in the political arena.

A number of deliberative polls have been held in Australia and these have been a rich source of learning for me. The first deliberative poll was in October 1999 on the issue of a republic, with the national referendum held the following month. Over 1,200 people were surveyed before a random and representative sample of 347 participated in the deliberative poll over three days. A second survey at the end of the process showed that the number in favour of a republic, those intending to vote yes in the referendum, had risen from 53 per cent to 73 per cent. On the question of a direct election of a president (with a people's vote rather than election by parliament) the number in favour fell from 50 per cent to 19 per cent.

Immediately after the results of the second survey were announced, those opposed to Australia becoming a republic, the monarchists, criticised the process of the deliberative poll, claiming, among other things, the swing to a yes vote was fake and that participants were brainwashed. I was there as a small group facilitator and didn't see any evidence of brainwashing. Still I couldn't help but wonder, if the vote had gone the other way and shown an increase in support for Australia remaining a monarchy, whether the republicans would have cried foul.

I facilitated in other deliberative polls over the next few years. One of these was on the issue of Aboriginal reconciliation. This showed a big shift in support for an apology to the Stolen Generation, but with caveats including any compensation being linked to demonstrated hardships. On the issue of a treaty between Indigenous and non-Indigenous Australians there was virtually no change in position.

One of the most surprising outcomes of a deliberative poll was on constitutional reform in South Australia. Here there was support for an increase in the number of upper house members. That's right, after a couple of days of a deliberative process, people wanted more politicians.

These outcomes suggest that given time and a process people are able to discern and evaluate different aspects of major issues and not just entirely throw their support one way or the other.

American writer F. Scott Fitzgerald said: 'The test of a first-rate intelligence is the ability to hold two opposed ideas in mind at the same time and still retain the ability to function,' to which I would add, 'while behaving in a civil manner.' Too many people have forgotten how to disagree without becoming disagreeable. In the age of social media some deliberately choose disagreeability.

People who have the opportunity to participate in deliberative processes consistently report their personal satisfaction, developing skills and confidences they hadn't known they possessed. Making an informed decision on a complex issue is liberating. It changes people.

They discover they like being an active citizen more than occasional visits to the ballot box.

I have experienced deliberative processes in a number of settings. This is a niche I feel comfortable in. It underlines my view that how people learn is often as important as what they learn.

2. Our departure from Sydney and the adventure of my employment at the Ideas Factory followed soon after the death of Meg's parents, six weeks apart. Shortly after this we had a trip to West Australia planned for a couple of weeks work on the trial of a falls prevention study circle for older people, with a short holiday to follow. A day or so before we were due to leave the world opened up. What, we wondered, was the point of coming back in late November when we had no commitments.

The return flight home was promptly cancelled and we gave ourselves a day to buy a second hand car to get around Perth, some regional areas and then home. With no timelines to worry about we did a five-week drift from Perth up to Exmouth and Coral Bay before heading south through Margaret River and out to Esperance and then across the Nullarbor. This was the perfect way to work through the death of Meg's parents and to debrief my experience in the Ideas Factory. Deciding each day what to do with that day is highly recommended.

Part of our time was spent pondering how to make a go of the business and find a way of feeling more at home in Jervis Bay, with a stronger connection with the community. We had often thought of the distinction between work and private time as being arbitrarily false. We didn't want a traditional work path and my experience in Sydney underlined the reasoning behind that. Obtaining local work became a goal and we achieved this with the local government contract I wrote of earlier, providing professional support to volunteer Bushcare groups. This contract, which we held for seven years, became a staple. Other occasional work came our way from Landcare, a local museum, a couple of community associations and the state housing department. All in all, things ticked along quite nicely and we blurred the distinction between our professional and private lives, mostly quite satisfactorily.

If the success of a business is judged by the extent to which the goals of the people involved were attained, we were a successful small business. John Howard was famous for saying small business was the engine room of the Australian economy, and I took to answering the phone with 'Engine Room.'

We had ample opportunity for professional development and took ourselves to a three-day workshop in Guided Autobiography. Sometimes known as Life Review, this program supports participants in small groups to share brief autobiographical life experiences based on themes, such as major turning points, family, career or passions. Although this has its roots in narrative therapy, it is not intended to be therapeutic any more than sharing life experiences with someone you trust can be therapeutic. This approach became a method I incorporated into much of the work I have done with groups.

I completed a recognised program in public participation, which had been a growing interest, hopeful of gaining occasional contract work in the area. In that respect I was almost entirely unsuccessful, though the skills I acquired became very useful in public life, which came to dominate a few years.

3. In 2005 a group of Huskisson residents formed a local community association, the Huskisson Woollamia Community Voice (HWCV); Woollamia being a small village on the perimeter of Huskisson. HWCV sought and was granted formal recognition as a consultative body by Shoalhaven City Council, one of 25 in the local government area. Being recognised meant council would actively seek the views of HWCV on a variety of policies and proposals. After this council would, at its discretion, ignore, dismiss or ridicule those views it did not like.

Council's attitude became apparent not long after HWCV came into existence when council released draft development plans for Huskisson.

HWCV coordinated a community response which was overwhelmingly against the proposed increase in height limits and development densities.

It was here that council's modus operandi quickly became apparent: first try to ignore, then dismiss and finally undermine, with the occasional personal attack as appropriate.

What started as a firm but polite rejection of council's plans, with absolute devotion to the truth and fairness, snowballed, in the way these things sometimes do, into a campaign to change the council. The snowball led to the formation of a new group in May 2007, the Shoalhaven Action Campaign (SAC). I stood down from the HWCV committee to focus on SAC where I took on the role of chairperson in September that year; one year from council elections.

The more you look the more you discover and many things were learnt about council's policies and procedures, or more to the point, the way council subverted these policies and procedures. This included the staples of poor local government, such as proposed sale of public land to favoured developers and the failure to declare political donations, but also some particularly creative attempts at hoodwinking the public.

Supporting a television guide masquerading as a newspaper (associated with a colleague of the dominant mayor) with advertising favourable to council was one. Aiming to provide generous additional communications expense reimbursement to councillors – a blatant re-election fund – was another.

Throughout the world it is common practice that those nations with three levels of government mandate for state government oversight and control of the local level. This helps to overcome the often narrow and parochial view of local councillors responding to their support base without recognition or understanding of the bigger issues involved. There were many instances of council breaching the Local Government Act and the state Department of Local Government regularly intervened.

Shoalhaven was a large local council, close to Sydney and with immense development pressure. In a nutshell there were millions upon millions to be made, which can bring out the worst in people. Throughout this time

I aimed to focus on the issues, and not the people involved, and mostly I managed to achieve this.

Submissions and meetings with state government ministers sought to have the council dismissed by the state government or at least have its planning powers for major development removed. Neither of these actions occurred but a campaign with broad community support in many areas – and strident opposition from some – saw major change at the elections of September 2008. The long dominant mayor lost that position and the majority of his supporters failed to be re-elected.

The Shoalhaven Action Campaign had come to dominate Meg and my lives. I don't want to beat my drum too much but I gave it everything and, combined with some quick on-the-job learning, put into practice all I knew about community organising, research and building a reliable media presence while canvassing for election candidates. Many of the beliefs and skills I had developed over the years towards political literacy and public engagement came to the fore. And I learned to look bullying in the eye and call a spade a spade.

From the outset I had never intended to stand for election, having a deep-seated belief that it was just not for me. I had a public profile and as the time came closer there was pressure to stand. I tried to talk myself into it but failed. A decision-making system based on numbers rather than reason did not sit well with me. The entire campaign that ran for a couple of years was not without its stresses and tensions. This was one of the hardest things I have ever done, but it was also one of the most rewarding things I have ever done.

4. Community associations are fraught with challenges. There is a widespread reluctance to join a committee with a common feeling that these are dreary, suffer from a lack of focus and inflamed passions. Some are run by cliques or pompous individuals who hold power close. And then there are internal power plays. Burnout is widespread. People give their all to a cause and then leave in disenchantment, or worse. This can apply to a sports club, a school P & C or a local charity. The challenges

become even more acute when there are contentious issues, and Huskisson was full of contention.

Following the council elections of 2008, and all that SAC had achieved, decisions had to be made. I needed time away from it and there were two clear options. One was to consider the job well done, with aims largely met, and decide to close down the association. The other was to continue at a more modest level than the frantic activity of the previous period. Unsurprisingly the second option was adopted. The thrill of the contest and the taste of success was too strong to set aside. Ultimately though, no one took up the mantle. A proud campaign withered away, became a memory, a faded gardening T-shirt.

A year or so later I returned to the HWCV committee, taking on the role of chairperson. I did a fair job of this but was regularly distracted by a couple of private projects that took much of my time. After a year I stood down and continued as an ordinary committee member, with more time to concentrate on the private projects. During this time I often spoke publicly, in my role with HWCV, on the continuing development issues. While the SAC campaign had made a major contribution to change within council, with seven new councillors out of 13, most of the new ones were just as supportive of big development.

Competition for committee membership of community groups is rare and HWCV was no exception. The following year I made it known I was happy to continue on the HWCV committee and expected to be able to put more energy into it, with the major personal projects out of the way. That was not to be however. At the annual general meeting it was clear an orchestrated approach had been hatched to see me off the committee. Appeasement with council was now the goal, and this was seen to be less likely with me involved.

Community work can be brutal. I pondered my response and ultimately decided to let it go, finding other ways to contribute. Surprisingly, Shoalhaven Council sponsored an Open Government Forum, inviting community contributions. I gave a presentation outlining transparency, accountability and participation. The forum was limited in its scope but preparing for this whetted the appetite and I made a commitment to do more. This led to a couple of well-attended public forums on local democracy and one on citizen journalism. These were based on my interests in building political literacy and community participation in local decision making. Public trust in democratic institutions is widely accepted as being in steep decline. I believe the local level offers great opportunities to re-engage people and reverse the decline.

Writing by instinct

Good writing has a style that reads, or sounds, like someone with a decent vocabulary, who uses it with creativity and originality and speaks well without sounding smart-arse clever. It is concise, not wasteful, clear, straightforward and does not overstate. It has liveliness, elegance and perhaps a rhythm. When read out loud it is engaging, very listenable. As American writer David Shields has said: 'Memoir is literature, not journalism.'

The rules of grammar many of us learnt at school taught us not to start sentences with 'and' or 'but.' But I disagree. So does Virginia Woolf who opened *A room of one's own*, first published in 1929, with 'But …' And, to support my point, a look at any contemporary nonfiction writing would reveal widespread use of these joining words (known as conjunctions) to start sentences. That's not to say all of the conventions of language usage should be ignored, rather a suggestion to know the rules before breaking them.

In a 1946 essay titled *Politics and the English language*, George Orwell talks of the importance of instinct in choosing words or phrases. Instinct, or intuition is how I write. I'm far more into feel, or sound of the word, sentence or paragraph than I am into the component parts of languages. I have little understanding of, or interest in, past participles or predicates.

Instinct, as in going with the first word or phrase that comes to mind has a lot to offer. But Orwell also acknowledges instinct sometimes fails and provided six simple rules for those times of failure. I have presented these below, with some additional thoughts.

1. Never use a metaphor, simile or other figure of speech which you are used to seeing in print.

A metaphor attaches words or phrases to things or actions that are not literally applicable. It perceives similarity in the dissimilar. 'His eyes were made of ice,' is one. 'It was raining cats and dogs,' is another.

A simile presents similarity by using the connecting words 'like' and 'as.' Such as 'he was strong, like an ox,' or 'she was as ferocious as an amazon.'

Be discerning, I would say, about clichés and the over-used words and phrases that lose impact through familiarity. Those that have been done to death (and that might be one) and are so commonly used as to seem hackneyed. While it is true a cliché can say in very few words what otherwise might take many, if the phrase is so general it can be used in a variety of situations, find another way of saying it.

'At the end of the day,' should be no-one's pride and joy. And there has to be something better than 'when push comes to shove,' or 'a magnificent sunset.' Aim for something original. I much prefer 'a bad day for the clouds,' to 'a cloudless sky.'

When writing about a character who uses clichés in their speech, for authenticity's sake, using them in their dialogue would be quite appropriate.

2. Never use a long word where a short one will do.

Is it better to *try* and do something, or *endeavour* to do it? Would you prefer the time or distance to be *approximate* or *about*?

Simple words are well suited to explain complexity. While it is possible to engage highly educated people with well-chosen year eight language, the reverse is far less likely.

Winston Churchill said it well: 'Short words are best and the old words when short are best of all.'

The more syllables the more abstract a word is likely to be. Stephen King, in his book *On Writing*, makes a point on short words citing a remarkable sentence of 50 words, none of which have more than two syllables, from a Steinbeck novel;

> Some of the owner men were kind because they hated what they had to do, and some of them were angry because they hated to be cruel, and some of them were cold because they had long ago found that one could not be an owner unless one were cold.
>
> **John Steinbeck,** *The Grapes of Wrath*

During a panel session at Byron Writer's Festival in 2019, prolific author Di Morrisey referred to her journalism training where she learnt to avoid big words that might demand too much of the reader. This is a maxim she follows in her novels. On the other hand, novelist and academic Gail Jones said she loves to come across the occasional new word. As with all things it's a matter of personal preference with regard to your audience.

In closing, on this matter, we might say, 'Notwithstanding these contrasting standpoints the ultimate decision is with the author.'

Or we might say, 'Be careful, but it's the author's choice.'

3. If it is possible to cut a word out, always cut it out.

Of course, no-one is perfect and Orwell demonstrates this with rule number three: 'If it is possible to cut a word out, always cut it out.' What he should have said is, 'If it is possible to cut a word out, always cut it.' There is no need to repeat 'out.' Or, I would say, to make an even sharper piece of writing, 'If it is possible to cut a word, do so.' But (cliché alert) who am I to quibble with a master?

'If I'd had longer it would have been shorter,' is an abridged version of an original quote, 'If I had more time, I would have written a shorter letter,' which has been attributed to numerous writers over several centuries.

The original source is not so important as the sentiment, which is that it is always possible to delete unnecessary words.

And it's true that the most over-used and unnecessary word that you could find is that word that. The previous sentence has two and arguably three unnecessary uses. I am accustomed to using it, and then deleting it during re-writes and edits. The 'Find' tool on the computer comes in handy.

We also use a lot of filler words. Words that take up space and apart from being unnecessary make writing less specific, murkier. Take, 'I heard the dog bark.' Of course the speaker of that sentence heard the dog bark. This is not in doubt, so why not, 'The dog barked.'

Similarly, 'I feel the sharp gravel on my bare feet,' is telling the reader something they know. 'The gravel is sharp on my feet,' credits the reader with a little more insight.

4. Never use the passive when you can use the active.

In the active voice, where the verb is active, the subject acts, as in 'Graeme loves Meg.' In the passive voice, where the verb is passive, the subject is acted upon, as in, 'Meg is loved by Graeme.' And 'I heard it through the grapevine,' is active and direct, rather than the passive and indirect, 'It was heard by me through the grapevine.'

In these two examples of the active voice the verb is active and the subject – *Graeme* or *I* – performs an action.

In the passive voice the verb is passive and the subject – *Meg* or *it* – is acted upon.

I wrote this book in fits and starts until I got serious, is active verb, active voice. This book was written in fits and starts until I got serious, is passive verb, passive voice.

'The cat ate the mouse,' is clearly active and more engaging than the passive 'the mouse was eaten by the cat.' But if you wanted to write from the perspective of the mouse, an intelligent animal, using the passive voice might do the job better.

Some people are pompous or overly verbose. Using a passive voice might demonstrate this character trait. And everyone has had one of those experiences when we are told, 'your call is important to us,' and then, 'your call has progressed through the queue.' Writing in the passive voice might show the tedium better. It can also bring variety and be a means to combine sentences.

5. Never use a foreign phrase, a scientific word, or a jargon word if you can think of an everyday English equivalent.

Knowledge is power, so the cliché goes. Hiding that knowledge in inaccessible language holds onto that power. 'Language,' it has been said by more than one person, 'is the chief means by which the professions conspire against the layperson and the general public.'

The earlier parts of this memoir are a story of psychological and moral growth from childhood through to adulthood and various phases between. Character development was (hopefully) evident. In literary terms it might be called a nonfiction *bildungsroman*. While there is joy to be found in a new word, everyone has their limit.

6. Break any of the rules sooner than say anything outright barbarous,
   Any rule that is more guideline than rule is my kind of rule.

The use and abuse of language

As a young person I liked writing and English was my best subject at school. Apart from a general tendency to dismiss adult advice, I can't explain to myself why I didn't consider a career counsellors suggestion of journalism. Much of my working life has involved producing community education and information material which usually included some form of a narrative approach. People will better remember the facts, or opinions of whoever is paying for the work, when they are embedded in a story. This approach helped immensely when I wrote on local politics. Along the way I learnt about the importance of language, including its uses and abuses.

Language can be used pleasingly with the aim of being readily understood, fair and engaging. Language like this can inspire, enthral and change lives. It can get you on the edge of your seat listening to a great speaker, have you glued to the pages of a great writer.

And it can be used in a dis-interested, mundane or leaden manner, pleasing only a bureaucracy. This is language to deaden the senses, have you looking at the clock on the wall, feeling pleased you borrowed rather than forked out for a book.

For the 15 years we lived at Jervis Bay on the NSW south coast, through until 2016, there was often talk of protection of some of the stunning views. One in particular was heavily dependent on a piece of prime real estate remaining as open space. Development ideas and plans came and went with a regular feature being the incorporation of a viewing platform, over one of the most sublime coastal views imaginable. Now if there's ever a literary surrender to the unimaginative, the utilitarian, the industrial, the functionalist, then viewing platform is it. Conjures up images of tourists disembarking the coach and being shepherded along the platform. In one end, follow the leader with the flag, take some photos and exit the other end: 'Come now, the bistro waits. And then the dolphin cruise.' Locals would learn when to visit to avoid the throngs. It could be so much better. A vista. An old-fashioned lookout even. In the great Australian tradition of a cockatoo being a lookout for illegal activities, maybe there was some inspiration from our avian friends. Perhaps there was an Indigenous word from the local area that could be applied. In Spanish it would be a mirador. Which makes my heart sing.

Language can be used honourably, to simplify and explain complex issues to a public that, in many areas, has largely come to distrust authorities. And it can be used dishonourably, with the intention of deceiving, hiding or manipulating. Knowingly leaving crucial facts out of a discussion is lying by omission. In 1992 the Australian government developed a *National Strategy for Ecologically Sustainable Development*. This defines ESD as, 'Using, conserving and enhancing the community's resources so that ecological processes, on which life depends, are maintained, and the total quality of life, now and in the future, can be increased.'

To the best of my recollection, sustainability was an uncommon or little used word before that time. Since then it has become popular and is widely co-opted. We hear of economically sustainable development. And, quite remarkably, there is an Australian Centre for Sustainable Mining Practices. There's a certain level of bombast when you claim sustainability for using something quicker than it is produced. Not to mention the waste that is produced and the unavoidable environmental impact of mining. Which is not to say I necessarily oppose mining, just that I support truth.

Whether intentional or not, language can obscure reality. Indigenous reconciliation is a case in point. It implies there was at some time in the past, a state of harmony, of goodwill – of conciliation – between Indigenous people and the colonisers. That there was no original dispute. Which is wrong. This falsehood might be addressed through a process of truth-telling about our history, as requested in the Uluru Statement from the Heart. Should a federal government ever have the courage. The Uluru Statement was developed in 2017 by a National Constitutional Convention of Aboriginal and Torres Strait islander people. It is, by the way, a lesson in poetics, plain speaking and honesty. I suspect some in-grained opposition to supporting Indigenous causes comes from being described as non-Indigenous. It cannot be helpful to be defined by what you are not.

Clouding an issue through obfuscation, or falsehood and leaving a way out of a prickly situation is the cornerstone of much official language. Among the Plain English Foundation's worst words of the year for 2019 was the phrase used by a Sydney engineer to describe a sinking apartment block as: 'moving in a downward motion.' A shining example of obfuscation.

A friend worked for many years in communications with a government department. As a true lover of words – a poet, a songwriter, a wordsmith – this was his forte, plain English was his specialty. And yet while he loved his profession, he hated his job. 'Government doesn't have a problem with plain English,' he says, 'they have a problem with the truth.' Many politicians have described people arriving by boat and seeking asylum in Australia as illegal arrivals. Which is a falsehood. No matter how people arrive to seek asylum they are not, by law, illegal.

Language can be used to build status, or elevate the ordinary to a higher plane. While studying horticulture, long ago, I learnt that plants were not to be called plants. Instead they were better known as 'plant material.' Took a while for the penny to drop but it was quite simple really. Creating specialist, or insider language gives status. At least it tries to. It excludes people who are not in on the game. At a base level it means you can charge more for plant material than you can for run of the mill plants. Much more recently I learnt that what blows around the planet, of its own accord, becomes not just wind but a wind resource. When there's money involved in using the wind that is. Similarly, rainfall becomes a rain event. Throughout this thirsty country councils have been busy installing water filling stations. They used to be called taps.

In 2007 Meg and I had a fun little project collecting and compiling stories of older people's experiences of the environment as they were growing up. This was published as *Stories of Experience*. Shortly after we were invited to present at a Sustainable Business Forum held at a Sydney university. Seemed an unlikely setting to talk about our project but we went along, describing our project as collecting and telling stories. Pure and simple. Later, over dinner at a nearby Thai, we wondered if, given the audience we were talking to, our work would have been better described as an: 'Open literary enquiry incorporating historical reference and lived experience.'

Simple language is widely touted as the best language, though clearly not everyone follows this advice. You can engage highly educated people with the language of a 12-year-old, but the reverse probably doesn't apply. While involved in a local political campaign on the NSW south coast I often struggled to find the right words to keep it accurate but simple. 'You're anti-development,' was the over-used but simple claim used against the campaign. Everyone's heard it. It sticks. Its proper rebuttal of: 'We aren't anti-development we support appropriate development,' asks the reader, or listener to concentrate. Maybe even think a little. The logical point to ponder is, what exactly is appropriate? And it's five words longer. A community campaign is playing catch-up in that argument straight away.

Language constantly evolves, with words truncating, compounding, coming out of nowhere, coming into or out of fashion. As a younger person I occupied myself by hanging around, either alone or in company. Nowadays the young don't hang around, they hang out.

Embedded within the language we use are our attitudes. Which can also change over time. Apart from being racist or sexist, language can also be ageist. In 2003 Meg and I worked on the development of a falls prevention program for older people. This is an important issue with serious repercussions for the elderly. During our work we unearthed a dichotomy. Young people fall over. Old people have a fall. At what age do young people stop falling over and start having a fall?

Sometimes the old terms stick fast. I have long been comfortable using the term black fellow to describe First Nations people. White fellow to describe others. Many older residents in the small country town where I live embrace political incorrectness, using the term darkie. 'The local darkies are okay,' they will say. 'It's the ones from elsewhere you have to worry about.' They may use this term in ignorance of its disparaging and racist tones. Or out of defiance. I can understand the dilemma for those stuck fast in the past, when they see it's now okay to call someone a black fellow, but not a darkie. Which doesn't mean I accept it. It's all to do with the heart, the empathy.

Average adult English speakers are said to have an active vocabulary of around 20,000 words, out of which we all have our favourites. The word fuck may be a favourite for many, it's certainly one of its most versatile, being a verb, adverb, adjective or noun.

Swearing has become normalised for many people, just a natural part of speech, with no intention to insult or offend. You may have noticed. Sometimes a swear word can even be a term of endearment, which may shock people not accustomed to this. Some years back I worked with a team on a land management project. One of the team and I were having a conversation in a meeting room one day about some aspect of the project. A conservation agency had produced a series of draft management plans for the area and these were on the table we were seated at. The cover of these used a series of photos, one of which was of local people. 'That's my brother,' he said pointing to one. 'He's dead now,' with a small choke in his voice, 'the fat cunt.' A much-loved brother I believe.

Workshops

In part one of this book I laid out the tale of how I came to be offering life writing workshops, starting in 2013. These have been rich experiences. I've never found them dull and have learnt something in every one. The best ones are those that challenge in some way. In 2020, while writing about these workshops, I noted: 'No-one has ever left early, or nodded off.' Which may have sounded a little smug. Certainly it was asking for trouble. I don't have to tell you what happened at the next workshop. Apart from that deep learning experience, here's some other reflections on these workshops that are mostly held in public libraries at an affordable cost.

I said earlier that my approach is that people can learn something from me, but they can learn more from and with each other. Downplaying the teacher-as-expert role supports the participatory nature of the workshop and builds confidence among the participants.

Learning from and with each other requires careful attention and practice in the art of giving and receiving feedback. Saying, 'I like that,' is not very helpful unless there is a teasing out of what it was that worked. In what way, for example, did the piece of writing reach out to other participants' personal experiences?

Likewise if something is not working, what is it that lets the piece down? In what ways can it be strengthened? When someone offers up a feeling about something that just doesn't quite feel right, but struggles to narrow it down, others can join in. When this goes well it's a joy to take a minor role, watching a cross-pollinating group working off their own energy.

One of my all-time favourites on the power of collaboration – learning from and with each other – was a small group in western NSW. A woman had much of the story of her grandparents, an Irish woman and an Italian man, and how they met on a boat to Australia after World War Two and fell in love. But she lacked an entry into the story. The small group unpacked the differences the woman and man must have experienced – no common language or food – before the writer came up with what I found to be a quite delightful metaphor: 'This is the story of the olive man and the potato woman, two people who met on a boat to Australia after World War Two, fell in love and became my grandparents.' I wouldn't say this writer was not going to find the metaphor in her own good time, but I'm quite certain that without the collaboration she wasn't going to find, and create it, on that day.

Along with a Senior's Card for my 60th birthday a few years back, I received a copy of *The Gift*, a book by Lewis Hyde first published in 1979. With a subtitle of *How the Creative Spirit Transforms the World*, the book is a defence of creativity in its many forms. It has many lessons, one of which is that whether someone is producing a painting or chiselling a stone, making music or penning a poem or a piece of prose, they are creating something new. It did not exist before they created it. And they should choose to look at this as a gift, firstly to themselves, and secondly to anyone they choose to share their creation with.

I started sharing this anecdote at the beginning of my workshops. I'm a pretty reasonable observer of participants and I'm quite certain this shifted something within their mindsets. They thought of themselves and their writing differently, with (particularly for those newer to writing) a higher regard for their creation. I always get quite a kick out of seeing confidence growing. This is part of the reason why I haven't gotten bored.

Although there are invariably those with quite strong skills, many of my participants have fairly low confidence in their writing ability. I've been a damaged learner, I've worked with damaged learners, and generally have an eye for those who arrive seeking the comfort of the (non-existent) back row. I use no technology and have only one insistence for the workshop, and this is that seating must be such that no one is looking at the back of someone's head. It's hard for people to learn from and with each, to be supportive, if eye contact isn't available.

⁓

As I have said, memoir comes from the word memory and not all memories are sweet. We all have our ups and downs, joys and traumas. Life writing can, and does, re-surface these memories.

Moist eyes are common in my workshops. I don't take it personally. One workshop created a record, when, during self-introductions at about the 12-minute mark, one of the participants was overcome and burst into tears. The whole group had a little discussion about life, writing on it and how it can affect people. It might not be without its re-lived traumas, but it can be cathartic. I thanked my teary participant for her honesty. Later on she thanked me. She didn't say it, but I'm certain she would extend the gratitude to the whole group that provided the quiet support she needed.

And then there are times where you can only wonder, such as my first early exit.

⁓

Expressionless she sat, face downturned. Seemingly reading, re-reading the handout. Occasionally twiddling a pen. But writing? Nothing. This was the first exercise of the writing workshop. Free writing. Pick up a pen, don't think too much, just write. Stream of consciousness if you like, keep the pen moving.

Clearly though, she was struggling. I tried to make eye contact, but failed. I would have liked the chance to talk, but that wasn't possible in this situation. I tossed out a line about some people who claim to need a plan before they are able to start writing. To which I invite them to write about why they need a plan. This too, to no avail.

I felt her floundering. Maybe, just maybe, I could sense her pain. She closed her notebook, preparing to leave, but in the small confined space we were using she was hemmed in. Then, when I called time on the exercise, less than 30 minutes into the three-hour workshop, she stood and left.

I have no knowledge of the circumstances of the woman who left early. I clearly recall greeting her on arrival, when she didn't want to chat to anyone but quickly took a seat.

There's an implied duty of care in these situations and the workshop organiser readily agreed to get in touch and check in with the woman. Just a small human contact which we all need sometimes. I hope she's OK.

On Show, don't [just] tell

'Show, don't tell' may well be the most widely quoted advice for writers. It means presenting an image rather than merely telling the reader what to think or what is happening.

Showing is sometimes known as scene. There is action or the promise of action or change. This may be dynamic, or it may be a subtle change in mood, emotion. It paints a picture, provides detail, relationships, significance and allows exploration. This leaves space for the imagination and invites the reader to see and feel the story and form their own conclusions, bringing life to the story. Think of this as the close up, a zoom lens.

Telling is sometimes known as summary. It is a statement of fact and may cover a relatively long period of time, presenting context or background, in a strong, concise voice. Summary may be within or between scenes, or in the same passage. Some telling is necessary in all but the shortest pieces. Think of this as the long view, a wide-angle lens.

We might tell someone: 'Barbara is an honest person.' Or we might show this by saying: 'Barbara has been known to walk a kilometre back to the shop to return the change she was overpaid.' In this simple example we are told something important about Barbara in five words and we are shown the same thing in 19 words.

This example illustrates an important distinction between showing and telling, showing takes more words. To justify the extra words there must be some value adding to the narrative. It might build tension or highlight character development or set up a situation, but if it doesn't do that then telling is the best option. Otherwise the tale will become overladen with insignificant detail, and way too long. Which is why I say Show, don't *just* tell.

If we wanted to tell something else along-side the 19 words that show Barbara's ethical stance, we might add a second passage to the first, as in: 'Barbara has been known to walk a kilometre back to the shop to return the change she was overpaid, though everyone knows she is keen on the sales assistant.'

Showing invites the reader to make connections or see patterns. It respects the reader and their ability to read between the lines and use their imagination. And with the exception of text books or instruction manuals, isn't that the joy of reading?

So how to show, rather than tell? There is a world of writerly advice on that, but the three elements of descriptive detail sensory language and dialogue will go a long way. Each of these have been covered earlier in this book.

> Consider the story told of a brief encounter with a stranger;
>> While walking along King Street Newtown one Saturday morning a woman, who I didn't know, asked me to carry two large bags across the road. I did this, surprised at the lightness of the bags. She wanted me to keep carrying the bags down the street but I wouldn't do this. I did, though, want her to thank me for my effort.
>
> Consider the same encounter, shown;
>> Ambling along King Street Newtown in inner Sydney, 10.30 on a Saturday morning. Joggers, coffee, designer dogs.
>>
>> A short squat woman, badly dressed and in need of a dentist, confronted me.

'Excuse me, you carry my bags across the road.' Feeling generous I viewed this as a form of request, the missing *please* an oversight. Two bulky cloth bags, I imagined of considerable weight, surprisingly not. I started to ask if she wanted to go down to the lights, not far away, and use the pedestrian crossing. Far safer I thought. But she was off into the traffic with me following. On the other side she kept going. I caught up. 'Here you go,' I said, placing the bags at her feet. She turned towards me then pointed in the direction she had been headed. 'Thank you,' I said to her blank face. And waited a second. 'Say thank you,' I insisted with a smile. 'Thank you,' she mumbled as I returned to ambling along King Street, Newtown.

The first two sentences are summary, telling the reader what they need to know of the setting. The second paragraph is scene, inviting the reader to form their own conclusions about the behaviour of the two people. It uses descriptive detail, sensory language and dialogue.

I wrote the essence of the encounter on a scrap of paper within a few minutes of it happening and tidied it up a couple of days later. Which is good writing practice. Or perhaps it's practising good writing. Showing rather than telling can be difficult to master, but once you get it, it makes the world of difference to your writing, bringing a zoom lens focus to a scene.

Self-portrait

In life there is luck. That is as true as anything can be true. Some luck is good, some not so good, some just plain terrible. You could say that two young Australian men, members of the so called Bali nine drug syndicate, who were executed in 2015, ten years after being convicted of their crime, had the terrible bad luck to be pawns in an Indonesian power struggle. Some say the Indonesian president, who had the power to stop the execution, saw more value in underlining his tough on drugs stance, despite these young men's excellent rehabilitation.

And you could say one of the suspected masterminds of that drug syndicate, who police have not been able to gather enough evidence against to charge, had some extraordinarily good luck. At about the time Andrew Chan and Myaran Sukamaran were sentenced to death he won more than five million dollars in the lottery, enabling him to give up drug smuggling. He settled for a comfortable life in suburban Sydney, apparently now living a law-abiding life. He may volunteer for charity and be a good neighbour. But luck like that, you imagine, must come with a price. How does he sleep?

And, so, where does luck fall? Apart from the good fortune to be born in a free country with some of the best services in the world, and an amazing natural environment, I was lucky to be born into a family where I never went hungry. I never knew deprivation or abuse, and had more than adequate resources. Perhaps I was a little less lucky in that family upbringing which provided no inspiration for the life to come. It was not a home of books, or music, conversation, or dreams. Benign neglect I have called it, with no disrespect to my parents who did the best they could with what they had available. And plenty had it far worse than me.

It's not easy for everyone, and for some it's exceedingly difficult, but you can make your own luck, and eventually, in a haphazard rather than planned sort of way, I started to do that. Getting away with a smart-arse response to authority provided the impetus, a springboard from where I started to find inspiration. Being open to opportunities is fundamental, a starting point. As is having a plan but being flexible and not being glued to that plan, not fearing failure. Better to go down the wrong street than stand on the corner. Though it helps to know your way back to the corner when it hits the fan.

Learning and transformation come from the negatives, the disappointments, the failures, and I have had plenty of those. I may have an over-developed capacity to cope with these. I know what I value. In thinking on where I have come from to where I am, there has been a transformation, both professionally and most importantly, personally.

I have suffered false friends, I have been a false friend.

Despite my regrets I am content. This is my default position. I have love in my life. I have a small number of special friends. I have health, adequate wealth, a home.

Yet there are times I feel an overwhelming grief. This can come from stories of child abuse, refugees in desperate plight, the wilful destruction of our natural world. And it comes from the back blocks of my memory, from the things I cannot change. I have long reconciled my familial relationships, my failings. Still, tears come unexpectedly, and I have to work on myself to regain control, to avoid being swept to a shadowy and sometimes dark place. Grief takes me deep inside myself, offering more insights than luck.

With a need for variety, change and movement in my surrounds I face a constant struggle to keep an inherent restlessness in check. I find stability in impermanence and manage feelings of never quite fitting in, wherever I live. Happy with the solitude of my own company, being self-contained with a need for few material goods.

I value the local, the communal, the recycled, the home-grown and hand-made. And the bigger stage. What happens in the world, or the local council, matters. And I don't mind whether it's community engagement in public policy development or street art, but I like it. I want more of it.

I believe in doing something for the community. That not everyone will appreciate what I do is a given.

I value the political process. I value it so much I would like to see it re-worked to be more accountable, more representative and fairer. Less accommodating to vested interests. This needs the ability and willingness to call-out knee-jerk responses and ideological positions masquerading as considered policy. And this capacity comes from critical thinking and open scepticism, but not cynicism. Never cynicism.

Equality and sustainability are admirable goals, even though these are more of a journey than a destination. We will never fully arrive. These things start with empathy, for people and planet. And civility. Being nice for the sake of being nice, being helpful for the sake of being helpful.

I like dogs, not cats.

I have a love of ideas. Nothing so practical as a good theory. If the occasional idea leads to something happening, that's a success, and the other ideas get filed away for another day. Which may never come. And I believe idealism is a much under-valued resource. If we can't visualise the best, how can we know what to accept, what to settle for?

I find joy and solace in nature, being happy in the sub-tropical rainforest near where I live, or the great grey plain of the outback, as Henry Lawson called the area on the far western NSW- Queensland border. A coral cay has value and appeal, same as a mudflat.

When it's all over I will die; I will not pass on.

From the Princess Room where most of this book has been written I look out to a grapevine, now setting fruit in early October, its new tendrils growing at a remarkable rate, reaching over the verandah to caress the native frangipani we planted five years ago and now seven metres tall. Last year it flowered so heavily the weight snapped some of the small branches. Remarkable.

Around this more fruit trees and vegies take prime position in our front garden and provide plenty for the table. There is much delight here. I look further to the west over the near distant hills, from where the summer electrical storms put on a show. And to the north, the Border Ranges part of the Gondwana Rainforests. Close enough for regular visits. I am lucky.

My luck really started in 1990 when I started in a job that built on my skills and experiences and offered plenty of scope to develop these. It opened up a world of possibilities. And, just a few days into the job I met Meg Bishop, who would become my best friend and lover. There is no more I could ask for.

More on memoir and life writing

Those readers who want to work on their own memoir may like to review the following sections throughout this book

	Page
On getting started	22
On narrative hooks	28
On sensory language	40
On point of view	87
On dialogue	124
On descriptive detail	142
On the personal essay	154
On Show, don't [just] tell	197

A Pocket Guide to Memoir Writing acts as a companion to this book. It is available at www.graemegibson.com.au

And while there are countless very worthwhile books on life writing I have found the following particularly helpful:

Brien, Donna Lee and Eades, Quinn (eds), *Offshoot; Contemporary Life Writing Methodologies and Practice,* UWA Publishing, 2018

Gornick, Vivian, *The Situation and the Story; The art of personal narrative,* Farrer, Straus and Girroux, 2001. E-book at https://oiipdf.com/the-situation-and-the-story-the-art-of-personal-narrative

Gutkind, Lee, *You can't make this stuff up,* Da Capo Press/Lifelong Books, 2012

King, Stephen, *On Writing; A Memoir of the Craft,* Hodder and Stoughton, 2000

Lamott, Anne, *Bird by Bird; Some instructions on writing and life,* Scribe, 2008

Miller, Patti, *Writing True Stories; The complete guide to writing autobiography, memoir, personal essay, biography, travel and creative nonfiction,* Allen & Unwin, 2017

Miller, Brenda and Paola, Suzanne, *Tell It Slant; Creating, Refining and Publishing Creative Nonfiction,* McGraw Hill, 2012

Moore, Dinty, (ed) *The Rose Metal Press Field Guide to Flash Nonfiction,* Rose Metal Press, 2012

Roach Smith, Marion, *The Memoir Project; A thoroughly non-standardized text for writing and life,* Grand Central Publishing, 2011

Rolls, Eric, *Celebration of the Senses,* Penguin, 1985

Tredinnick, Mark, *The Little Red Writing Book,* UNSW Press, 2006

Zinser, William, *Writing About Your Life; A Journey into the Past,* Da Capo Press, 2004

Sources
Part One

Page

1   Patti Miller, 'Life writing is inclusive …' See https://lifestories.com.au/

4   Ruth Park's novels, *The Harp in the South* and *Poor Man's Orange,* were originally published by Angus & Robertson in 1948 and 1949 respectively, with many reprints since

4   E.M. Forster, *Aspects of the novel,* Edward Arnold, 1927. Electronic edition published 2002 by RosettaBooks, https://www.rosettaebooks.com/ebook/aspects-of-the-novel/

5   Dinty Moore, *Gotham Writers: Inside Writing – Flash Nonfiction,* Season 2, Episode 10, https://m.youtube.com/watch?v=sGelRGHCKaM

6   M. Bishop & G. Gibson (eds), *Stories of Experience: Learning from the environmental experiences of older Australians,* Council on the Ageing (NSW), 2008

8   E.L. Doctorow, 'Writing is like driving at night in the fog,' in *Writers At Work: The Paris Review Interviews,* https://www.goodreads.com/work/quotes/622615-writers-at-work-the-paris-review-interviews-2nd-series

8   Richard Ford, *Canada,* Bloomsbury, 2012

9   Vivian Gornick, *The Situation and the Story; The art of personal narrative,* Farrer, Straus and Girroux, 2001. E-book at https://oiipdf.com/the-situation-and-the-story-the-art-of-personal-narrative

11	Bruce Springsteen, in Michael Hainey, *Beneath the Surface of Bruce Springsteen*, November 27, 2018, https://www.esquire.com/entertainment/a25133821/bruce-springsteen-interview-netflix-broadway-2018/
13	Lee Gutkind, *You can't make this stuff up*, Da Capo Press/Lifelong Books, 2012
15	Robert Dessaix, 'Essays will be read in 500 years …' *Letters to an Unknown Friend,* Australian Book Review, June 2010
16	For more on flash nonfiction, see: Dinty W. Moore (ed) *The Rose Metal Press Field Guide to Writing Flash Nonfiction,* Rose Metal Press, 2012
18	Graeme Gibson, *Beyond Fear and Loathing: Local politics at work,* More Than Just Talk, 2012
19	For introductory information about the need for legal advice, Australian Society of Authors, https://www.asauthors.org/search?command=search&search_terms=legal+advice
20	D.B.C. Pierre, *Release the Bats: Writing Your Way Out Of It,* Allen & Unwin, 2016
22	Lewis Hyde, *The Gift: Creativity and the Artist in the Modern World,* Vintage Books, 2007 (first published 1979)
22	Mihaly Csikszentmihalyi, on 'Flow,' https://www.ted.com/talks/mihaly_csikszentmihalyi_flow_the_secret_to_happiness?language=en

Part Two

Page

25	Marion Roach Smith, 'Memoir requires transcendence. …' *The Memoir Project: A thoroughly non-standardized text for writing and life,* Grand Central Publishing, 2011
29	Robert Dessaix, *A Mother's Disgrace,* Flamingo, 1994
29	Anh Do, *The Happiest Refugee,* Allen & Unwin, 2010
30	Robyn Davidson, *Tracks,* Vintage, 1992
30	Clive James, *Unreliable Memoirs,* Jonathan Cape, 1980

30	Bert Facey, *A Fortunate Life,* Penguin, 1981
30	Kim Mahood, *Craft for a Dry Lake,* Anchor, 2000
31	Raimond Gaita, *Romulus, My Father,* Text, 1998
34	Negativity bias, https://en.wikipedia.org/wiki/Negativity_bias
35	Marion Roach Smith, *The Memoir Project: A thoroughly non-standardized text for writing and life,* Grand Central Publishing, 2011
39	Child abuse and adult offending, https://aifs.gov.au/cfca/bibliography/child-abuse-and-adult-offending
41	Eric Rolls, *Celebration of the Senses,* Penguin, 1985
56	Youth Justice Conferencing, https://www.youthjustice.dcj.nsw.gov.au/Pages/youth-justice/conferencing/conferencing.aspx
58	Gordon Elias Gibson, minor misdemeanour and crimes:
	The Advertiser, February 6, 1926, https://trove.nla.gov.au/newspaper/article/132048678?searchTerm=Gordon%20Elias%20Gibson
	The Advertiser, July 20, 1929, https://trove.nla.gov.au/newspaper/article/73757334?searchTerm=Gordon%20Elias%20Gibson
	The Advertiser, March 5, 1936, https://trove.nla.gov.au/newspaper/article/129265502?searchTerm=Gordon%20Elias%20Gibson
64	Uluru Statement from the Heart, https://ulurustatement.org/the-statement
65	Justice Reinvestment, https://www.justreinvest.org.au
71	HOLLYWOOD'S LOVELIEST WOMEN, Australian Women's Weekly, April 6, 1955, https://trove.nla.gov.au/newspaper/article/51597247
73	Bertrand Russell, https://www.goodreads.com/quotes/878848-the-trouble-with-the-world-is-that-the-stupid-are
74	Domestic violence, Northern *NSW District Data Profile: Mid North Coast, New England and Northern NSW,* NSW Department of Families and Community Services, https://www.facs.nsw.gov.au/download?file=725850
	Socio-economic disadvantage, *Kyogle Local Government Area, Fact Sheet,* North Coast Primary Health Network, https://hnc.org.au/
77	Kristen Roupenian, *Cat Person,* The New Yorker, December 4, 2017 https://www.newyorker.com/magazine/2017/12/11/cat-person

103	America's opioid crisis: how prescription drugs sparked a national trauma, October 25, 2017, https://www.theguardian.com/us-news/2017/oct/25/americas-opioid-crisis-how-prescription-drugs-sparked-a-national-trauma

Part Three

Page

115	Ralph Waldo Emerson, 'A man must consider…' In Webster's Electronic Quotebase, ed. Keith Mohler, 1994. At: https://quotable-success.com/products/view/128330/A-man-must
130	Human Rights and Equal Opportunity Commission, *Bringing them home: Report of the National Inquiry into the Separation of Aboriginal and Torres Strait Islander Children from Their Families,* https://humanrights.gov.au/sites/default/files/content/pdf/social_justice/bringing_the_home_report.pdf
132	2008: National Apology to the Stolen Generation, https://www.nma.gov.au/defining-moments/resources/national-apology
132	2009: National Apology to Forgotten Australians and former child migrants, https://www.nma.gov.au/defining-moments/resources/national-apology-to-forgotten-australians-and-former-child-migrants
137	1990 National Landcare Program, https://landcareaustralia.org.au/project/thirty-years-of-caring-for-our-country-the-landcare-story/
141	Paulo Friere, *Pedagogy of the Oppressed,* Penguin, 1972
142	Ira Shor, *Critical Teaching and Everyday Life,* South End Press, 1980
145	Fran Peavey, *Strategic Questioning Manual. A Powerful Tool for Personal and Social Change,* https://commonslibrary.org/strategic-questioning/
145	Focused Conversation Method, https://www.top-network.org/use-focused-conversation
148	Joseph Joubert, https://en.wikiquote.org/wiki/Joseph_Joubert
149	Chatham House Rules, https://www.chathamhouse.org/about-us/chatham-house-rule
149	Graeme A Taylor, *The Australian wine industry: is the glass half full or half empty?* Mt Eliza Business School, June 2001

149	Harvard Business School, *GE's Two Decade Transformation: Jack Welch's Leadership,* January, 2000
149	Peter, Laurence & Hull, Raymond, *The Peter Principle: Why Things Always Go Wrong,* William Morrow, 1969
151	Paul Radley, *Jack Rivers and Me,* Allen & Unwin, 1981
	Australian Bureau of Statistics, '2021 Census shows changes in Australia's religious diversity,' Media release 28/06/2022, https://www.abs.gov.au/media-centre/media-releases/2021-census-shows-changes-australias-religious-diversity
153	Ipsos, Global Views on Religion, 2017, https://www.ipsos.com/sites/default/files/ct/news/documents/2017-10/globaladvisor_Religion_Charts_AUSTRALIA.pdf
154	Karl Marx, full quote in context: https://yourstory.com/2017/05/quotes-by-karl-marx
154	Lucius Annaeus Seneca, more on: https://www.newworldencyclopedia.org/entry/Seneca
154	Aristotle's persuasive rhetoric, https://blog.ed.ted.com/2017/01/17/rhetoric-101-the-art-of-persuasive-speech/
156	Bob Boughton, personal communication, quoted in: Graeme Gibson, *Beyond Fear and Loathing: Local politics at work,* More Than Just Talk, 2012
157	Kate Krinks, 'Creating the Active Citizen? Recent Developments in Civics Education,' Parliament of Australia, 1999, https://www.aph.gov.au/About_Parliament/Parliamentary_Departments/Parliamentary_Library/pubs/rp/rp9899/99RP15#Major
166	Graeme Gibson, 'Another Ride On the Youth Engagement Merry-Go-Round,' New Matilda, June 2014, https://newmatilda.com/2014/06/16/another-ride-youth-engagement-merry-go-round/
173	Apprehended Personal Violence Order, https://www.bocsar.nsw.gov.au/
177	James Fishkin, 'Why Deliberative Polling?' https://cdd.stanford.edu/mm/2017/09/naver-oped.pdf
177	Stanford Center on Democracy, Development and the Rule of Law, 'Deliberative Polling on the Referendum to make Australia a Republic,' https://cdd.stanford.edu/1999/deliberative-polling-on-the-referendum-to-make-australia-a-republic/

	ABC Radio, AM, 'Claims of bias in republic poll,' Transcript 25 October, 1999, https://www.abc.net.au/am/stories/s61691.htm
178	F. Scott Fitzgerald, https://www.brainyquote.com/quotes/f_scott_fitzgerald_100572
184	David Shields, *Reality hunger: a manifesto,* Vintage/ Random House, New York, 2011
184	Virginia Woolf, *A room of one's own,* Hogarth Press, 1930
184	George Orwell, *Politics and the English language,* 1946, https://www.orwellfoundation.com/the-orwell-foundation/orwell/essays-and-other-works/politics-and-the-english-language/
191	Plain English Foundation, https://www.plainenglishfoundation.com/worst-words
194	Graeme Gibson, 'The gift: On writing workshops,' *Northerly,* Byron Writers Festival, Spring 2020
195	Lewis Hyde, *The Gift: Creativity and the Artist in the Modern World,* Vintage Books, 2007 (first published 1979)
199	Nick McKenzie, Richard Baker and Michael Bachelard, 'Suspected Bali Nine mastermind living in luxury' as Andrew Chan and Myuran Sukumaran sit on death row,' *Sydney Morning Herald,* February 10, 2015, https://www.smh.com.au/national/suspected-bali-nine-mastermind-living-in-luxury-as-andrew-chan-and-myuran-sukumaran-sit-on-death-row-20150210-13aypt.html

Final Word

Thanks for reading *In Life There is Luck*. As an independent author I rely on word-of-mouth recommendations and I would greatly appreciate your rating and/or review. If you enjoyed it please consider writing a review and posting it on online retailers such as Amazon, Goodreads, or your own blog.

To subscribe for updates or to find other information please visit my website www.graemegibson.com.au

If you are part of a book club looking for an author to meet with you via videoconference or in person I would be happy to talk with you about writing and publishing. Please feel free to contact me through:

Facebook	www.facebook.com/Graeme3GibsonWriter
Twitter	@Graeme3Gibson
Instagram	graeme3gibson

Find my Blog at:
www.graemegibson.com.au

www.ingramcontent.com/pod-product-compliance
Lightning Source LLC
Chambersburg PA
CBHW032035290426
44110CB00012B/809